Stop, Drop, Grow, & Glow

Holly Swenson

Stop, Drop, Grow, & Glow

Cover Photo Credit: Dee Dee Designs
Photo of four boys taken by Sarah Stivers
Family & author photos taken by Shannon Edney Photograph

ISBNs:
Paperback: 978-1-950476-72-5
Hardcover: 978-1-950476-73-2
Audiobook: 978-1-950476-75-6
eBook: 978-1-950476-74-9

This book is dedicated to my husband Tom, my always & forever;
my four boys, my infinite gurus and the little loves of my life;
to all parents walking the path of parenthood, you are the change.

Praise for Stop, Drop, Grow, & Glow

"If you are looking for a friend and guide to help you navigate parenthood, look no further! Holly Swenson provides a framework for conscious parenting that aligns mind, body, spirit, and environment in a way that will enable you to nurture your family, practice self-care, and create a peaceful and loving home."
-Susan Pohlman, author of *Halfway to Each Other: How a Year in Italy Brought Our Family Home* and *A Time to Seek: Meaning, Purpose, and Spirituality at Midlife*

"*Stop, Drop, Grow, & Glow* is full of inspiration and is very uplifting. Holly's wisdom comes from her passion and dedication as a mother. This book has been written from the heart and is rich of insights and guidance at the spiritual, medical, and psychological level. It will support any parents and grandparents on their journey."
-Tejpal, MA, MBA, author of *Manifest Moment to Moment & Way to Be*

"Holly Swenson gives us lessons for living on the planet as more conscious parents, partners, and community. What a gift—to be able to raise a new generation of self-aware and loving children. Thank you, Holly, for sharing your insightful wisdom and generous spirit. I loved every word of *Stop, Drop, Grow, & Glow*'s hopeful, inspiring message."
-Susan O'Connor, coeditor of *Hearth* and *The Wide Open,* cofounder of Families First Boston and Families First Missoula

"If only Holly Swenson's invaluable guidance was within reach when I endeavored to be the most dedicated single dad on the planet. Every chapter brought a smile to my face as I relived the happiest years of my life."
-John McCaslin, journalist and author

"*Stop, Drop, Grow, & Glow* is a framework that combines Holly Swenson's nursing background, personal development, open heart, and lived experience of the mother of four into an actionable set of tools (my favorite is the Five Rights Of Parenting) to help find and keep centered on parenting with intention and love. It is a solid addition to the mindful parenting landscape."
-Elke Govertsen, CEO and Publisher of *Mamalode*

"Holly has crafted a wake-up call for all parents to be brave enough to dig into the "why" of who they are as a parent. She opens a path for love and compassion for yourself and your children, with practical tips on how to do both."
-Amy Pelloquin, M.D.

"This book, if you take the energy to integrate its philosophy into your daily routine, can be a game changer. It encourages reflection, gratitude, and self-growth/forgiveness. As an occupational therapist, it is an important reminder to remember differences to build tolerance, so we all can glow."
-Kay Kramer, OTR/L, CHT

"Holly Swenson provides a beautiful and realistic guideline with tangible takeaways into becoming a more conscious parent so that you can act in alignment rather than fight a battle. By sharing her personal stories, she allows us to feel that we are not alone in our journey and provides space for us to personally dive deeper after every chapter."
-Dr. Emily S. Jacobs, nurse, coach, speaker, and author of *Live Your Life For You (Not Your Mom)*

Letter From The Author

Stop, Drop, Grow, & Glow will revolutionize the way you parent. This book is truly a companion for child rearing. Within, you will find tools and wisdom on how to infuse consciousness into your everyday life, help you make deeper connections with yourself and your family, and teach you how important it is to not lose "you" in the process of raising your children. This book will set you on the path for deep personal insights and help you identify the parts of you that may be wounded and in need of a tune up or healing. It will help illuminate your journey of what it means to fully embody being a conscious parent. The ultimate premise of this book is to provide a road map of how to parent with consciousness. I write this as an offering to the world in the hope that it will help other parents on their journey and allow for more happiness and joy in raising a family. Writing this book has been a reminder for me to parent with mindfulness and intention, while honoring my own needs as a mother and individual. I have been encouraged to up my game as a mom and really live what I speak to.

Unveiling this conscious parenting book is a long-awaited dream of mine, so I thank you for your time and attention as you turn the pages and receive what it is I have to offer. My hope is that it will provide you with what you seek. I am not a licensed therapist, nor a doctor. I am a woman, wife, mother, registered nurse, and seeker of knowledge on the path of parenting and life. I am called to share my truths as I feel them, know them, have experienced them, and witnessed them in the world. The information contained in this book is an offering from my heart to yours, so do with it what you will. Please take care and consult a health care professional or licensed therapist before making any alterations in your diet, exercise regimen, parenting strategy, and the like. You know you best, so always proceed with what feels appropriate to you and to your family. You are indeed the master of your universe.

Table of Contents

Introduction

Years ago, when my children were still very little, I was given a sign that read, "Mothers work from son up to son down." At the time I thought that was a sweet message and put it in my kitchen, where it continues to sit to this day. This has been a daily reminder of what it takes to rear children, and let me tell you, that sweet sign is surely accurate. I am the mother of four boys who truly keep me working from son up to son down. I love my boys more than life itself. They are my total joy, my biggest teachers in life, hard work, and at times the bringers of pain in what it means to be a parent. There are many growing pains in fully embodying what it means to be a parent and the work and learning is seemingly never done. Tomorrow always brings something new to the table and you never can quite guess what package it will come in. In this book, I will illuminate a path of better parenting and provide a framework I call the Stop, Drop, Grow, & Glow Method. These tools can assist you in effective and more joyful parenting, as you walk side-by-side with your child, teaching one another in this miracle we call life. I have acquired much wisdom along the path of parenthood I want to share to make this world a brighter and more grounded place to raise our young. Let's get to it and re-imagine what parenting is.

PART 1

STOP

Chapter 1: Self-Reflection

"Children are not only innocent and curious but also optimistic and joyful and essentially happy. They are in short everything adults wish they could be." - Carolyn Haywood

"Twins! You are going to have twins!" My husband and I looked at each other in the doctor's office and both started to grin. We had just started trying for a family and boom, right out of the gates we were starting big. We were immediately overcome with joy and excitement for what was coming our way. The gift of parenthood times two. Such a blessing was bestowed upon us both in that instant. Two beautiful boys. The miracle of stirring life staring back at us from the ultrasound machine. This is how my parenthood journey began; a moment in time I will forever cherish. After the birth of our twins we then went on to have two more beautiful boys; one twelve months later, and our fourth son, three years after that. The sweetness and sacredness of family is everything and has helped me grow in ways I never imagined possible.

With the sweetness of family, there are also moments of saltiness, with hurdles to overcome and navigate. As a parent, learning to find your joy spot somewhere in the middle of the yin and yang of sweet and salty will help you thrive in the process of child rearing. Not only are you raising your children, but ultimately you are inadvertently raising yourself at the same time, whether you realize it or not. Parenting is beautiful, but it is also hard work and doesn't always unfold the way you think it will. It is important to consider how you are parenting, but it is equally important to examine how well you are tending to yourself in the process, as this will directly affect how you show up for the ones in your life.

How well have you been captaining your parenting ship up to this point? If parenting is proving to be more than you bargained for, or overwhelming in ways you couldn't imagine, then the Stop, Drop, Grow, & Glow Method will change your life.

Sometimes life asks you to slam on the brakes and evaluate how things are going, and as parents we often override this ask in the busyness of life. Right now is the perfect opportunity to take a deep look at your role as a parent and the role your child plays. Observe where there may be holes or spaces that need to be mended or made whole. Like the wasps mend their paper hives when damaged, consider doing the same in your own home. **Stop** and tap in. Take stock of dynamics, habits, patterns, and joys. When you get quiet is when you really can listen and gain the clarity you need to move forward in a dynamic and healthy way.

When you **stop** and self-reflect, you can actually slow down enough to listen to what your heart already knows. Your heart is a major wisdom center, so don't be afraid to use it. Learn to hone your emotional intelligence and let your heart lead the way. Your heart is a magnificent guide in life, especially in regard to parenting. Remember to occasionally turn off your mind and deep dive into your heart. Your mind can get busy, messy, and be a space of distraction at times. Give that beautiful and wild mind time to take a rest every now and then. There is nothing wrong with that.

If there are things you are doing really well and are having great success with, keep it up! Well done. If you have areas that are not how you want them to be, it's time to get real with yourself and others (perhaps family members) about how you want to take positive steps to form an unbreakable family foundation. Thinking about how you want things to be is not enough. You need to take action to make the shifts you so desire. Ideally, you must be all in, halfway won't get the job done.

However, recognize the shifts you may desire as a parent

won't change overnight, you have to practice patience with yourself as you work to come into better alignment. This takes time. My aim in this step of the Stop, Drop, Grow, & Glow Method is to help you learn how to **stop** and assess early so that potential parenting pitfalls can be avoided. While there will be unforeseen challenges we all must face as part of the parenthood initiation, with more intentional living and daily work done on your part, parenting will be a softer and more joyful place to land.

STOP

- **S**: Stress…Change this to "yes I can."
- **T**: Time (or lack thereof)…Shift this thought pattern to "time is what I make it."
- **O**: Obstacles…Think of obstacles as your teachers, make them your ally.
- **P**: Pressure…Adjust this reality or perception to patience and loving persistence.

WAKE UP CALL

About seven years ago, I hit a wall. I had four young children at the time (ages one, four, and twins that were five) and had experienced a difficult year. That year brought with it a serious illness for me–meningitis–that had me hospitalized for about a week, from which I thankfully recovered. However, at the time I genuinely thought my life might be over. I remember lying in the hospital bed telling my husband I felt like I was dying. It was a very surreal experience and a big wake-up call. Not only did I have meningitis, but unbeknown to me initially, I was leaking CSF (cerebral spinal fluid) from where they had done the diagnostic spinal tap to check and see if I had meningitis upon admission. This wasn't discovered until a couple of days after I was hospitalized.

I remember lying there and being totally with it, but feeling like I was having an out of body experience. Once the leak was discovered, they were able to do what is called a "blood patch" to seal it. I immediately felt better and began improving, but the first night after getting home from the hospital I could actually feel my brain touching both sides of my skull when I would walk or move. This is a memory I do not care to relive. I never thought I would be staring my mortality right in the face at such a young age. Despite this experience, I was fortunate, and went on to make a full recovery.

A couple of months after my ordeal in the hospital, my stepmother passed away unexpectedly, which was devastating. She was such a beloved and bright light for our family and our community. It happened so suddenly that there wasn't time to properly say goodbye, so living with the reality she was gone was a tough pill to swallow. This was another major wake-up call, as I deeply realized the preciousness of our time here on Earth. Every day is indeed a gift, and yet oftentimes you forget as you get bogged down with life's requests and demands, many of which are out of your control.

These are just two experiences to draw from that year which had me feeling at max capacity and really re-evaluating my priorities in life, not to mention the day-to-day challenge of raising four little boys. I finally hit a point where I told my husband I needed to get away for a few days. This request ultimately led me to find Miraval, a wellness retreat in Arizona. I remember getting on the plane the day of departure, trying to get my luggage in the overhead compartment, and even that felt overwhelming. Something so simple had me on the verge of tears. My whole body was full of tension, and I felt tightness everywhere. I was at my personal limit with how much I could take on and was finally realizing that. Once I landed and arrived in the desert, I was able to finally take a long-awaited, extended exhale. One thing I realized almost immediately upon arrival is the quietude of being alone. I had not taken a trip alone since my kids were born and had forgotten, or maybe never even realized before this point, how important it is to find silence and stillness, especially when you are child rearing. I spent my time at Miraval practicing self-care and nourishing my mind, body, and spirit in ways I had never done before. It was a life altering experience to say the least.

There is something so magical and healing about the desert. Miraval has continued to be a place of respite for me over the years since that first trip.

My three days there forever helped reshape my perceptions of life, including the need for intentional living and self-care. I had a major realization of how important it is to slow down and tap into stillness more. It was my first **stop** and self-reflect point on the roadmap of where I was and where I was headed, both as an individual and as a mother. Oftentimes, it is the stormy seasons of life that bring the most personal change and teach us how to sail on smoother waters with purpose. I believe this with my whole heart. Now is the perfect opportunity for you to look within and do some real-time, real-hearted evaluation.

DO THE WORK

I invite you to **stop** right now, self-assess, and self-diagnose how you are doing as a parent. When was the last time you stopped to consider where you are at and where you are going? There is no better time than *right now*. **Stop** and write down or contemplate how things are going and ways you might authentically evaluate family, your life, and lifestyle. Are there any challenges you are facing or limitations that are keeping you from living your best parenting life? Curl up with these questions, get deeply honest with yourself, and take stock.

HONESTY

What is the truth of the parenting situation you are currently in? I appreciate the word honesty because it allows for vulnerability and unearthing of truth as you search within yourself for where you are now. Not where you've been, or where you are going in the future, but where you are today, right now, as you read these words. When you get honest with yourself and don't sugarcoat your parenting experience, like perhaps you do for the outside world, you allow room for consciousness, authenticity, healing, and growth to start taking root. This means being aware if you have been living on autopilot. For example, if others ask you how you are doing and you instinctively say, "great!" when you might be in a space that is feeling anything but great, you aren't living in true alignment.

There is disharmony and that will alter your reality until you can **stop** and personally realign yourself. Benjamin Franklin said it best when he said, "honesty is the best policy" and surely it stands here. All of this starts with getting honest with yourself. If you can't be honest with yourself and do some real soul searching, how do you intend to grow and continually improve as a parent and as an individual? This is a crucial step in the stopping phase. Sometimes over the course of parenting we learn how to wear masks or put on a front that is not the real version of who we are, much less how we want to show up for our children, others, and ourselves. When you can right yourself, it makes it much easier to right other relationships in your life as well.

For years I've wanted to write a book but kept putting it off because I kept asking myself, *what do you know about parenting, and who are you to tell others how to parent?* Some days I felt like I was nailing parenting and others…not so much. The days I wasn't hitting the mark further cemented my belief pattern that I wasn't the woman for the job. However, as I've gotten farther down the parenting path, what has become clear as day is that there is no such thing as a perfect parent. We all make mistakes, we all say things we wish we could unsay, we all sometimes yell at our kids and wish we hadn't, we all are learning, and we all need to go easier on ourselves and on our children.

I have finally reached a point in life where I feel I can really be honest with myself, and there is freedom in that. Be proud of the steps you take, even the imperfect steps, and remember to parent with honesty, integrity, and sincerity. Be proud of you. You are enough and you have enough to give. You are perfectly imperfect.

SURRENDER

Surrender has become one of my favorite practices as a parent. It is an incredibly humbling experience to raise children, and I've learned over the years that sometimes the best choice is to surrender to what is. I have a type-A personality, so this is not something that comes easily or naturally to me and is something I have had to be more intentional about as a mother. When you let life unfold without trying to manipulate outcomes or appearances, there will be more ease to the process. Surrendering is not an effortless practice, as many of us have been shaped by a society that tells us otherwise. It takes work and mindfulness to remember.

Something that has been a constant work in progress for me, and an area in which I continue to actively practice surrender, is letting go control of my home environment. I have tendencies towards striving for perfection, and really love having my environment feel good, i.e., dishes done, house cleaned up, things in their place. A lot of this stems from having an inconsistent home base when I was a child, so I work hard to meet certain needs, but this habit doesn't always serve me in the best way. For example, sometimes I will prioritize cleaning the kitchen in the evening instead of sitting and playing a game with our kids. When I **stop** and think about this pattern, I realize the kitchen can wait. What needs shifting is how I show up and respond to my children's needs while meeting my own, and how I prioritize meeting those needs, if the day and circumstances allow. You only get so many opportunities to play games with your kids while they are young–you get to wash dishes the rest of your life! Take any opportunity you can to play with your children. This doesn't mean you should neglect the household responsibilities or needs you have because I am a firm believer in cleanliness, but strike a balance. If there is a tendency you lean towards, try to bring it back to the midline. Find the happy medium. Perhaps try to complete this work when your children are not at home, before they wake up or once they have gone to bed, or even seek outside help if that's an option, so it takes some of the pressure off of you.

It is also helpful to remember this isn't about parenting perfection, it's about parenting practice. When you strive for perfection, you will fail every time. I am not perfect, and this will not come as a surprise, neither are you or your children. We are all continually learning and growing, that is what this journey is all about. Some days it might get messy. Lean into that and learn from it. Let your parenting ego go and surrender more so that you can parent from a space of less reaction.

Once you can take your parenting ego down to the nuts and bolts, you can really start parenting in a more authentic way that allows more spaciousness for you and your child. Letting go more can make room for letting more in.

It is easy to get wound tight as a parent. Some days it feels like you are in a pressure cooker and there just aren't enough hours in the day to complete the 101 things that need to get done.

Instead of shooting for perfection or beating yourself up for not meeting every need or demand perfectly, look for ways to release some of this pressure and proceed with more joy and ease. Allow room in your life for mistakes and set reasonable goals. Don't stack up too many tasks or commitments that are unrealistic to meet because this will likely lead to feelings of personal inadequacy or irritation for not being able to complete all you set out to accomplish. Set yourself up for success and remember to **stop** and touch base with what this looks like for you in your life.

Further, I urge you to focus on significance over perfection; what is the meaning and depth of what you are choosing to do and is it meaningful to your life personally or your family? The meaning behind what you do is important, so make sure you are choosing things in life that are in alignment with what you want to be doing. If the tasks are taking away from your experience as a parent, make a shift and bring it back to your center point, so you can keep your priorities straight and bring as much joy to your experience as possible. Finally, take a look at your tendencies and have more awareness here. When you understand what makes you tick and can recognize where you might feel constricted, you can start to release any tendencies that aren't helping. If you don't take the time to look, you might not find what you are looking for.

With four boys as roommates, my needs and their needs don't always mesh or align the way I hope they might. I have a tendency to clean more than I should for them because it is something that soothes me. I also can get cranky when there are messes lying around, such as wet towels on bedroom floors, so I have to be mindful of how I step into a situation, as it is ever changing and requires a lot of patience and consciousness. I believe if you want to change habituated patterns that are not helping you on your journey, you must name them and hold them up to the light. Really own and claim what is taking away from your true essence so you can begin to get a handle on it. This will be time well spent.

One of my more painful surrendering stories occurred after the birth of our fourth son. I had my hands beyond full when our children were little because we started with twins, and twelve months later we had our third son, so in many ways it felt like having triplets. With this many babies, I needed a triple stroller that could handle the situation. We had a royal blue stroller that was my life saver when they were little, and we took many a walk in that thing. With the arrival of our fourth, we ran out of seats. The youngest got to ride shotgun in my momma pouch (infant carrier, front side), while I pushed the other three. One afternoon, I headed out for a walk with my children and also needed to walk our two dogs at the same time, so I grabbed their respective leashes and bags and we all set out for a walk. Little did I know this walk would end up being another big turning point for me.

We live near a college campus and were walking on the main sidewalk when a skateboarder came zipping by, and our large, young dog lunged to chase after him. I was able to stop our dog thankfully, but in doing so I almost fell with our brand new baby, and almost tipped the stroller over. The crisis was averted, but it was a seriously close call. Freaked out by this experience, I turned around and headed home. A couple of blocks from home, our dog again lunged, this time at a squirrel, and the same scene played out. After I had finally arrived home, got all the boys out of the stroller and settled, I sat down and cried.

This big, beautiful dog we loved so much was more than I could handle at that point in my life. The realization was staring me straight in the eyes. I didn't have the time or capacity to care for so many other beings in the way I wanted to. My dog was acting out because he needed more one on one time and room to roam. I just didn't have enough time to tend to him the way he needed amongst the juggling act of caring for four little ones. I also realized I wasn't willing to risk getting one of my children injured in the process of trying to meet our dog's needs. Dogs had always been my universe before kids, but something happens after childbirth and your children then take center stage.

Luckily, I shared this story with a family friend who said she would love to take him in and make him their beloved pet. They had everything that was perfect for our dog; plenty of time to spend with him, no children, and acres to run on. It ended up being a happy change for our dog, which I will forever be grateful for. It was the right choice for us at that point in life, but a difficult one. Two weeks after this emotional transition of letting our beloved family dog go, our other dog who had watched me grow up passed away from old age.

This was the ending of an era, and a time of total surrender. I was heartbroken in so many ways and also worried about what it would look like from an outsider's perspective. *Would we be judged for giving our dog away? Who does that?* I always wanted my children to have dogs, and what had transpired was not the story I had written in my mind. This experience asked me to surrender and just walk through the flame, so that's what I did. Surrendering in this experience ultimately led to better outcomes for all. It wasn't what I wanted, but I knew it was what needed to happen for all parties involved.

How can we invite more surrender into our daily lives? Often surrendering is seen as weakness, when in fact it is one of the most empowering, brave, uplifting, and grounding experiences we can have as human beings. When we surrender our hearts, our minds, and our spirits to what is–exactly as it is, without expectation–we can find peace. This creates breathing room, allowing for inner movement and inner harmony. It can open the door to living an authentic and peaceful life. Surrender puts you in a state of meeting yourself exactly where you are. This is a beautiful place to be and allows for life to ebb and flow in a way that is more organic and natural. I invite you to explore what surrender means in your life and how it might feel to let life happen around you for a day or even an afternoon without judgment, without being stuck in your mind or caught up in what you think it should be. Surrender and carve out a space that is filled with intention and acceptance of life exactly as it is, especially when it comes to your family.

HUMBLED

Having children will humble you from root to crown. Literally every inch of your being will be made humble in the process of child rearing. Let it. There is so much out of your control in the process of raising your child and so many things that happen whether you want them to or not. You have to learn to be okay with what is, not what you want it to be or what you think it should look like. Releasing attachment to your ego will be of maximum benefit on this journey, but not an easy or comfortable thing to lay down, that's for sure. Many of us wear our ego like our favorite sweater, tight and snug. Try taking it off, you might just find freedom and spaciousness waiting for you.

Humility is another one of my favorite practices as a mother. Lay down your pride and be open to learning and being schooled in different ways; you might be surprised at what your children can teach you. Remember, some of the lessons you learn will be incredible and some will be tough. They all work in union to help shape and shift your soul.

I have a memory of being humbled while traveling when our boys were younger. Since we have six people in our family, it has always worked well for us to get an entire row on planes. I was in the middle seat on one side and my husband was in the middle seat on the other side (with two kids on either side of us). On this particular trip, one of our children got sick to his stomach, which is a rarity in our family. It happened to be on my husband's side, and before he knew what had happened, our son had thrown up and he instinctively made his hands into a bowl shape, catching most of it. We looked at each other dumbfounded, horrified, and unsure of where to go from there.

Passengers in nearby seats were obviously grossed out and shocked. I scrambled to assist my husband with the cleanup and tending to our son in tandem. We got things back on track quickly and made the rest of the trip without further incident. This is one of those memories we can laugh about now, but in the moment, it was a seriously humbling experience to be in the center of something uncomfortable publicly, but doing our best as parents to remedy whatever situation we might find ourselves in. It is moments like these along the path of parenting that will help you to not take things too seriously, especially when many of these realities are out of your control. It can help you as a parent to practice what being humble means, becoming less self-involved, and more sensitive to the practice of parenting and to the feelings of your children and others.

CONSCIOUS PARENTING

You might be wondering at this point, what is conscious parenting? What does that even mean? Merriam Webster's definition of consciousness reads, "The quality or state of being aware, especially within oneself." I would take this a step further to include that it is an awareness of both internal and external experience. This means you have an awareness of what is going on inside of you and what is happening around you in the world. I'm not going to define parenting because I'm quite sure if you are reading this you are well aware at this point what being a parent entails. Merging consciousness with raising your children is my definition of conscious parenting.

Part of tapping into consciousness is learning to **stop** and allow yourself to gain perspective on any situation at hand. The act of stopping and practicing self-reflection allows for greater clarity on familial matters that might need more attention, and other areas that maybe need less or can be ignored all together. Maximizing your time when you have so little time to spare as a parent takes intention and practice. Reflecting on lessons learned, ways to improve your role as a parent, current situations that are adding to or taking away from your joy factor, and achieving more consciousness among the chaos are all things to **stop** and ponder here.

To add a layer of physicality to the stopping process, I also offer some suggestions so you can feel the **stop** in your physical body and deep in your bones.

- Stop moving, get still, and put two hands over your heart or belly, as these are both big energy centers in your body.
- Take a seat, close your eyes and count to 20, or use a calming mantra as simple as, "I am peace," or, "loving

kindness."

- Tap your fingertips one at a time to your thumb and repeat several times.
- Bring your palms together and hold them at your heart center or third eye (your forehead). I personally like to envision holding a lotus or beautiful flower at my heart and sometimes will hold my palms together (down near my wrist creases) and fan my fingers out so that it looks like I am holding a flower. This helps me to remember my sweetness and quickly return home to myself.
- Lions' breath can be a great release if you are experiencing tension or want to alleviate stress (search for this on YouTube if you aren't familiar with this). It looks a little silly, so you may prefer to do this one at home in the company of your child, who probably will give you a sideways glance and giggle at you. Perhaps invite them to breathe like a lion too.
- Wear a mala, which is traditionally 108 beads in a necklace or bracelet form that is intended to help you focus your mind during meditation. This is a great physical reminder to have on your person throughout your day. I will delve further into 'reminders' in a later chapter.

You can always come up with your own version of what it

means to physically **stop**, these are just a few ideas to help kick-start the journey.

GUILT

The guilt people feel as mothers and fathers, whether they choose to be stay-at-home parents or re-join the work force right after the birth of their child can be enormous. When I got pregnant with twins, I worked three twelve-hour night shifts per week at our local hospital. I loved my job and my co-workers, but my husband and I made the decision that I would stay at home with our sons and be there to raise our family. This is a decision I have never regretted, and something I will always be grateful I had the opportunity to do.

I recall shortly after the birth of our twins we would be out in our community, and when we'd run into acquaintances I would often be asked, "are you still working?" This was a question that made me feel less than, because I had given up my position as a registered nurse to focus on the home front. I wanted to shout, "yes!" I've never worked harder, but being a parent doesn't seem to carry the same respect as a nine to five job, which is truly a shame. So instead, I would smile and say, "I am not currently working, but I am staying home with our children." Upon reflecting further I've realized this was my own issue. I truly don't believe any offense was meant by the well-intentioned friends trying to make small talk. However, every time I was asked that question it made me feel like I wasn't doing enough as a woman or as a parent.

I did attempt to go back to the hospital and work part-time about three months after our twins were born, but my mother-in-law who was going to help us with the boys ended up having a massive heart attack about a week after I started back. With this major shift in life events, I decided to pull away from work altogether. It just wasn't in the cards for me at that point in my life. I also discovered about the same time that I was pregnant again with our third son, so the path forward seemed obvious–I needed to stay the course being home for my family.

While I had feelings of insecurity for a time after quitting my job at the hospital to be with our boys, I was able to replace those feelings with gratitude and knowing that I am enough and am doing enough. Once I shifted my perspective, I was able to start living and parenting from a different vantage point, one that felt whole and complete. I stopped worrying so much about what my life looked like from an outside perspective and put my energy into what it felt like to be living it. But first, I had to **stop**. Conversely, if you are feeling insecure about going back to work after having a child, try to work to find gratitude and joy in knowing you are providing for your family and doing work that matters. While many parents are grateful to be able to stay at home after the birth of their child, there are also many parents who are happy to return to their job. In fact, I have heard many parents voice over the years that it is easier to go to work than stay at home with their kids. They love their children but look forward to breaking up the day with other responsibilities and continuing their professional growth. Some parents love being at home with their children, some do not. Neither is right or wrong, they are simply different. Try to shift the lens to meet yourself wherever you are in life.

Take time to **stop** and see where you may be holding guilt surrounding parenting, whether it be that you are staying home with your children, or that you are a working parent and not able to be with your children as much as you think you should be or want to be. This feeling can materialize and play tricks on you, so don't fall victim to the G-word. I realize the deep privilege I've had to be a stay-at-home mom while raising my children and respect this isn't the case or reality for many parents out there.

Guilt is one of those emotions that can easily seep into your life, so be mindful here to remain grateful for whatever course you are currently on, and walk your path with gratitude, knowing you are doing the best you can with what you have. Regardless of what path you are on or have been traveling, do not let guilt permeate your experience. Parenthood is precious and a serious journey no matter where you are, where you've been, or where you are headed. Parenting, like life, will look and feel a little different for everyone.

THE ACT OF STOPPING

The actual act of stopping is not an easy task to take on. What parent has the time to stop and evaluate what is working and what might not be working in their personal life or in their child rearing? I certainly didn't believe I had time for this when my children were little. I was busy chasing my boys around making sure everyone was staying safe and being fed, napped, walked, or changed. It was a constant grind and left little time for extracurriculars. However, had I known back then that it doesn't take all that much time and effort to tap in and make room for more conscious parenting, I would have slowed down and practiced this evaluation much more often, which would have made my experience more joyful and less exhausting. One step at a time. **Stop**.

REFLECT

1. Have you ever stopped to check in with yourself since you started your parenting journey? If not, what are you finding out about yourself now that you are pausing a moment to take inventory?

2. Does stopping and checking in with yourself feel challenging? Stressful? Nourishing? Selfish? Take a moment here to self-reflect on emotions that may or may not be arising.

3. Do you think stopping and doing some internal gazing will benefit your parenting, why or why not?

Chapter 2: Five Rights of Parenting

"Parenthood…it's about guiding the next generation, and forgiving the last." - Peter Krause

I am formally trained as a nurse (BSN, RN). With this knowledge comes responsibility; responsibility that I am proud of. There is something called the five rights of medication administration that is utilized in the clinical setting. These are as follows:

1. Right patient
2. Right medication
3. Right time
4. Right dose
5. Right route

Following these five rights helps to ensure that as a nurse, you are doing the right thing for your patient and not causing harm. These are simple, straightforward, and fairly easy to commit to your memory bank for recall. I went to college for four years to earn my Bachelor of Science degree in nursing, and I will forever be grateful for the time and energy I invested in reaching that goal. Those four years and my professional title deemed me proficient to work as a nurse in the clinical setting. Nurses are amazing humans who work tirelessly for their patients and communities. I could go on and on here, but this book is about parents, who also work tirelessly for their children, but in a different way.

I want to make two vital comparisons. The first being with many professions, there is a minimum of four years education to be considered proficient in a given trade. With parenting, you might have been lucky enough to have a brief stint in high school health class that touched on family planning or maybe you had to carry a doll or an egg around for a week and report back. I didn't even receive that education. Instead of preparing our parents to be, we push them off the deep end and say, "start swimming!" OMG. How unprepared are so many parents when starting a family? This is the most important job there is, and yet we don't prioritize as a society the education and understanding of what child rearing is and is not. There is virtually no preparation, and many new parents have little to no support or understanding of a more conscious and joyful way to parent. How unfortunate for all the new parents and all our new little ones being born into this human soup of confusion. Still, many successfully adapt and figure it out as they go, doing the best they can. Humans are so resilient and incredible in this way.

The second comparison I want to make is the model of the five rights of medication administration and putting a parenting spin on it. I want to offer a supportive parenting protocol I've created, called the *Five Rights of Parenting*. They are designed to help you **stop** and check in with yourself on how you are showing up for your child. They are as follows:

1. Right Now
2. Right Intent
3. Right Use of Speech
4. Right Use of Power
5. Right Use of Love

The *Five Rights of Parenting* are designed to be a quick way to touch base with yourself on how you are presenting as a parent. Just like with patients, these five rights also work to ensure you are doing the right thing and not causing unnecessary harm to your child (or yourself) in the process of parenting. This should be used daily or as often as you can remember to reconnect with yourself and assess how it's going. Every day is going to be different, but how you show up for your kids doesn't have to be so variable. The other piece here is that it doesn't matter your background, financial status, race, culture, or creed; all parents could use support and guidance. We all want what's best for the next generation; this is a universal and innate desire around the world, in every walk of life. Let's make this child rearing process as beautiful as we can across the planet so the next generation can thrive and live with more awareness and grace.

Right Now speaks to being in the moment and present for your children. Not texting, not working on three other things while your child is asking for your time and attention. When you show up for your child, really show up and be all in for them. It will teach them how to be present for others and will ultimately set them on a path to success in their future relationships. The tightest bond they will have is with their parents in their formative years, so make this bond the strongest and most beautiful bond you can. There are no repeats here and time is ever fleeting, so maximize the precious time you have and make sure to live in the moment with them. There is no second place to being in the present. Your child will blossom from knowing they are your priority and worthy of your time. If you truly cannot put aside what you are doing, give your child a hug and set a time to connect when you find a place to take a break. Looking back, you will be glad you made this a top priority.

Right Intent is showing up for your child intentionally. Being intentional in how you treat them, the choices you make, the guidelines you set, and the framework you use to parent. If you don't know why you are doing what you are doing, it's time to re-evaluate your parenting strategy. Knowing your reasons for your actions and decisions is key to being an intentional parent. When you become intentional in your life, doors start to open in healthy ways with your child and beyond. If there are doors that are not open with your child or otherwise, try being more intentional with what you are doing and see if this helps shift things in a positive direction that can set you on a new course. Write about ways you can or want to be more intentional, steps you are willing to take, or perhaps seek out a professional that might help you on your way–such as a life coach. Focus on bringing that intention into your life daily. Walk your talk and start living it.

Right Use of Speech is a critical component of effective parenting. How you speak to your child is one of the most important aspects of raising your young. Your voice is a tool of creation and thus has the power to create a positive or negative mood. This also can be one of the toughest rights to remember to implement. *Right Use of Speech* takes a lot of practice and consciousness to remember, especially if you have more than one child. It can be easy to get swept up in your child's situation, mood swings, or meltdown and forget to use the right language to reset. If you get swept out to sea with your child and you both are speaking the language of crazy, who is steering the ship? Think about this one! Some days this will happen regardless of your best intentions, but the more you practice speaking with awareness, the easier it will become to start from a rooted and solid foundation. Practice, practice, practice, and have compassion for yourself when you don't meet the mark. We are all learning all the time, regardless of our age.

The *Right Use of Power* is a big one. As a parent, you are the guiding light for your child. You are the one who wields power, decides on discipline, sets boundaries, and you have the final say on whatever issue may arise along the long road of 18 years, until they get to start doing this for themselves. With this power comes big responsibility so use it wisely and with care. Do not abuse this power or manipulate your authority in this role. You need to be firm in creating a safety net with clear boundaries, but be mindful of how you apply your power. Perform an honest, internal check-in here on where you are at and if it is being helpful or if it is being hurtful. There is a clear distinction, and you know in your heart of hearts which category it falls into.

Right Use of Love is by far my favorite Right. I believe love is the cure for all that ails us, parenting and beyond. This right should be used as many times a day as you can aspire to. Letting your child know how much you love them and are there for them will help them plant their spirit and childhood in deep, rich soil as they grow. Be careful not to use love as a reward or in a way that is not authentically given. Love isn't a prize to be won, but rather a gift from your heart to theirs.

One thing I have had to learn in life, though not necessarily related to love, is to give without expectation. Love is one of those things that should be given away without the need for reciprocity. Your children likely will mirror the love you give them, but if they don't (especially as they get older and are going through puberty), keep giving that love. They are receiving it and aware. Giving love matters and it makes a difference, even if it goes unspoken.

REFLECT

1. Journal about how prepared you felt having a child. Are there areas you want to learn more about related to parenting?

2. What is your plan for implementing the *Five Rights of Parenting* in your life?

3. Are there any of the *Five Rights of Parenting* that feel difficult to embrace or utilize in your family? If so, which ones and why?

CHAPTER 3: RESPONSE VS. REACTION

"Every time you are tempted to react in the same old way, ask if you want to be a prisoner of the past or a pioneer of the future."
- Deepak Chopra

One day when my twins were toddlers, I went to get them up from a nap. They shared a room when they were little and oftentimes when they would wake up from a nap they would be chattering away, saying cute things to each other or playing. This particular day when I went to collect them, I opened the door to an absolute disaster. They had pulled the blinds off the wall, dismantled their beds, taken their diapers filled with number two's off, and had absolutely trashed the joint. I was horrified and did not show up the way I should have.

I needed to **stop**, but instead I said, "okay, you boys are no longer sharing a room." I immediately started moving one bed out of the room into another and didn't stop the moving of items until there was total separation. From that day forward, they no longer were roommates. After I was done moving them, I was exhausted and exasperated. If I had stopped and taken time for self-reflection, I likely would have approached the situation with more care and more tenderness, instead of jumping right in and leading with reaction. I would have taken a moment to breathe, had them help me clean up the room, talked to them about how to make better choices, let them continue to be roomies, thrown them in a bubble bath, and could have turned this into more of a teaching moment. Ultimately, this would have been a better response because it would have allowed me to **stop** and be much more intentional. Oh, to have redo's in life!

How can you **stop** reacting and learn to respond? With practice and commitment. At the center of all charge is a state of purity. We build layer upon layer as we grow and sometimes these layers get so thick, we can't remember who we are at our core. This is especially true after having children. When we are prioritizing everyone around us and often neglecting ourselves in the process, we have a tendency to lose some of our identity. If your identity has been fractured in the process of child rearing, **stop** and take time to remember who you are and what brings you delight.

If you are living with anger, anxiety, depression, or feelings that can be overwhelming for you and your family, spend time reflecting on how you got to this point, perhaps by journaling it or sharing what's on your heart with a licensed therapist. Search for any triggering events in life, points along your journey where you didn't have the support you needed, or didn't have parents to teach you what it means to be loved and respected as a child. Also, consider any trauma, violence, or addiction issues that may be at play here, as well. Take a moment to remember who and where you are in life. Do not skip this step, because when you remember how to fill your cup, nurture your own spirit, and mend the parts of you in need of mending, you will be better able to serve those around you.

I have a curious mind and always appreciate learning new things and different ways of being. At different points along the path of parenting I have often wondered, *did the Buddha have children? How would an enlightened being raise a child? How can you find your center in the madness of raising kids?* It sounds like a great idea, but holy sh*t. This work is arduous and takes everything I have and more to keep the train on the tracks some days. What I have learned over time, by taking moments to **stop** and reflect, is that the madness is the teaching. All those sticky, hard spots are exactly what I was meant to learn from and work through. Once I started to realize that surrendering to the hard parts on the path is what helps me to learn and grow, it enabled me to have more compassion for myself and for other parents as well. When I resist and try to control the sticky parts, I don't do my job as well and I am definitely not as effective.

This also has taught me that when I am out and I see parents struggling with their child, instead of passively offering judgment, I should instead **stop** and silently offer them support and love because I know what it takes to keep at it, day in and day out. Instead of judging another's parenting style, offer compassion or a helping hand if the situation allows. The moment of weakness you might be witnessing in another, you've likely experienced yourself. Cultivate a spirit of understanding here. It takes fierce determination, incredible stamina, and a big heart to keep at it relentlessly. **Stop** and remember that parents are warriors. Keep your heart open and keep the compassion flowing, both to yourself on your own parenting journey and to others. I have learned over the years that it truly does take a village to child rear, so strive to be part of the solution.

REACTION

Reaction is all too easy to ignite when raising your child. When you react to your young, you are shooting right back to them whatever they are offering. Reacting is immediate and usually not thought out. Often parents have to make snap decisions and don't have the luxury to really think about how to optimally reply to a request, action, or naughty behavior. Frustration or feelings of being overwhelmed can take over, and you might bark out some orders or say something you might later regret because you were reacting in the moment, and you forgot how to proceed with care. I will raise my hand here and say that I have fallen into this category many a day while raising my children. It is easy to react and even easier to forget to **stop**, breathe, and consider how to lovingly help whatever situation you find yourself in. Reacting is an instinctual drive, so this is a hard one to conquer.

When your child is having a tough time and acting out, don't be afraid to hold space for them when they need it. When they are throwing a tantrum, don't join them and have one too. Instead, work to standby in a non-reactionary and supportive way that allows them to expel their intense feelings so they can return to their own homeostasis. If you join in their tornado, you are only going to magnify the problem and become much less effective at leading your child out of their emotional storm. If your typical approach to your child having a tantrum is to scold them, **stop**, give them a hug, and get quiet instead. Lay down the rollercoaster of emotions. You both will feel the difference and most likely will both benefit from a softer place to land.

RESPONSE

Response on the other hand, requires more processing, thought, intention, and time. It allows for emotions to cool or breathe, and there is more awareness of your own experience as well as how you approach different circumstances. Responding is more deliberate and considerate in nature and can produce much healthier and more balanced results in relationships, especially the parent-child relationship. Responding is more thoughtful whereas reacting is much rasher and less thought out.

In fact, when you react, there is no pause to process because it is innate. For this reason, reacting is much easier to utilize as a means of defense and survival because it is instinctual. It is what is there waiting for you, helping you survive, but sometimes those survival instincts do more harm than good. There also is an element of reaction stemming from conditioned responses from your own parents or society, many of which tend to be negative. When you can remember to respond, it allows for you to **stop**, process, remember your manners, intent, and leadership skills as a parent, so you can move forward in a healthy and dynamic way, rather than a battering ram just pushing through to the next task trying to survive.

My boys used to watch *Daniel Tiger's Neighborhood,* an animated program for preschoolers that is essentially a spin-off of

Mister Rogers' Neighborhood, when they were little, and there was a line from that children's show that for whatever reason has stuck with me. "When you feel so mad that you want to roar, take a deep breath and count to four." I have used this to remind myself and have also encouraged our boys to use it because it is easily relatable to kids and easy to remember.

Often your child is a little ball of reaction, so it's important you both have tools to draw from when you need them the most. When you start parenting with response rather than reaction, it will improve your social skills, and allow for more self-awareness, self-regulation, and empathy. Responding also will open the door for you to start witnessing your own motivation behind how you communicate and act towards those around you. Don't forget, when your child witnesses you using these tools, you are modeling healthy behavior for them which will support them in a more optimal manner. There is room for tremendous growth here if you allow it, so be sure to water your personal flower rooted in response regularly, and watch it bloom beautifully.

DIVORCE

While we are on the topic of reaction versus response, it seems like the perfect time to segway into talking about the D-word. Divorce is an all-too-common occurrence for parents and children alike, and I believe in many instances this stems from living in a reactionary state. I am a product of divorced parents and learned to walk this walk at a young age. It's not an easy road for either those getting divorced or the children who are left to pick up the pieces in the aftermath. Being a parent in a loving, committed marriage has given me a lot of perspective on what I didn't know or receive growing up.

In 2022, the divorce rate according to the CDC was 2.3 per 1,000. To look a little closer at the numbers: there were 1,676,911 marriages (the marriage rate was 5.1 per 1,000 total population) and the number of divorces was 630,505. This means roughly 45% of marriages ended in divorce. This rate is actually on the decline compared to previous years, but you also have to factor in an important component: the marriage rate is also on the decline. Baby boomers (those born between 1946-1964) are the most likely to get divorced, which I found interesting because I would not have guessed that to be the case.

Pew Research notes that because baby boomers had an unprecedented exposure to divorce at an early age, it then led to instability in their own marriages later in life. In fact, *The Washington Post* had an interesting article that further says, "The wisdom about divorce in America goes something like this: the sexual revolution sparked a sharp rise in the divorce rate from 1950 until about 1980, leading to the famous formulation that half of all American marriages would end in uncoupling, conscious or otherwise. But in the 1980's, the divorce rate began to decline," (Ingraham, 2021). I also wonder if perhaps part of the causality for this higher divorce rate is that many baby boomers really redefined traditional values and were oftentimes freer spirited than their predecessors.

The newer generations, on the other hand, have many more tools at their disposal and more support and encouragement than ever before. Millennials (those born 1981-1996) are waiting longer to get married and have become pickier on who they are willing to settle down with. There is more focus on education and financial security before starting a family, and they generally approach marriage and family life much differently than previous generations (Stepler, 2020).

The primary causes of divorce are arguing, infidelity, commitment challenges, marrying too young, financial problems, domestic abuse, religious differences, substance abuse, and little or no premarital education (Scott, 2013). As I read through this list of top patterns that lead to failure in a marriage, I noticed they all seemed to arise from living in an unconscious manner except, perhaps, financial struggles. I personally believe that divorce most often stems from unconscious living and existing in a state of reaction versus response. I feel many people are never taught how to be conscious, how to properly care for one another, or how to properly attend to themselves. They perhaps didn't have great role models as children, and potentially witnessed heavy dysfunction within their childhood homes, and then perpetuated the problem once they decided to start a family. This cycle of dysfunction keeps feeding itself, unless you wake up to recognize it, address it, and choose to walk a more grounded path. If this section is striking a chord, this is the point where you **stop**.

One of the new buzz words related to divorce these days is "conscious uncoupling." This term came on the scene in 2009 and was coined by Katherine Woodward Thomas, essentially meaning couples who choose to separate still work to maintain their mutual respect for one another. They don't villainize each other; they maintain integrity, work to prioritize their children, and practice self-reflection to prevent repeating the same pattern in the future (Goop, n.d.). I love that more consciousness has been infused into how couples are choosing to disengage with one another, as it ultimately benefits them both personally, while honoring any children that might be impacted as well. I extend big kudos to all those parents out there who are facing the decision to walk away from a relationship that isn't working for one reason or another and are choosing to start anew with more courtesy and care than ever before.

I offer an additional thought about "conscious uncoupling" in the opposite direction and suggest that we put the same or more effort into conscious coupling, meaning we take the time daily to care for ourselves and those we keep as our beloved. Being in a committed relationship is a living, breathing, dynamic partnership in its own right (separate from the relationship you have with your child) and one that needs to be lovingly and consciously tended. If we fuse the relationships or try to merge them all into one big relationship, things can get messy, and the lines can become blurred. You deserve to first and foremost have a grounded, thoughtful, loving, and clear foundation with your significant other. It's from this base that you can bring a family into the mix with a clearer direction in which your family chooses to go. Being conscious of your partner means that you are intentional and care about each other's needs, desires, pursuits, dreams, happiness, and hold one another's hearts like you would a newborn. This process allows you to prioritize needs appropriately and connect with each other on a deeper level. Take care and make sure you are tending to the flame of commitment and are both working at this partnership. If only one person is committed and trying to do the work for both parties, it just won't work for the long haul, and if it does endure, it could foster a breeding ground for dysfunction to take root. This dynamic might work in the short term, but won't foster a healthy or optimal foundation, especially after starting a family. Additionally, be mindful of the relationships you choose to keep, and make sure they are reciprocating the work you are putting in. Reciprocity should be a two-way street, as this is what will keep a relationship thriving and proving beneficial for both recipients.

You also need to make sure you aren't putting your children above your significant other or using your children as pawns in the relationship. There should be clear leadership and love at the top, as in you and your partner, or perhaps just you. Your children need that clarity to trickle down to them, so they understand their role in a healthy and dynamic family. Your child needs to be your child, and they need clear communication and boundaries on what this looks and feels like.

Remember, it will be different in every family. Your children might be your greatest loves and biggest joys–and rightfully so–but in a marriage or committed relationship, you need to make sure your children don't become your total focus, causing you to lose sight of caring for your partner's needs. Both relationships are separate and therefore require different tending.

One last thought here is that while you need to support both relationships in different ways, there is an additional relationship you tend that falls under the family bubble–what I call the family triad. In the family triad, you tend to all three relationships simultaneously. There is the spouse-spouse, parent-child, and spouse-child-family. You will recognize each of these relationships if you spend time looking closer and reflecting when you have one-on-one time with your partner, one-on-one time with your child, and when you all are together. Look for any differences and similarities and aim to strengthen any of these relationship dynamics that may feel strained or be off in some manner.

An example of how I bring this to life in our family is related to tending to the spouse-child-family relationship, also known as the family triad. We prioritize having at least one meal together as a team per day (usually dinner), as this is our time to tend to one another and do some daily processing. It allows us to all come together and be intentional with how we check in with each other. One of my favorite ways to ask my husband and our boys how their day has been is to play the game *rose, bud, thorn*. The rose refers to the best part of their day, the bud signifying anything that was learned or something that they are interested in knowing more about, and the thorn being anything they faced that was difficult or challenging. This opens the door for real sharing, growth, processing, and support from the whole family. It is intentional and it is mindful in helping one another feel heard, valued, witnessed, and supported on their path. This is a gift we give one another, and it means so very much. It is also an opportunity for us all to collectively tend to one another and touch base daily to keep the foundation strong.

Finally, if you are not currently in a committed relationship and are going it alone, keep these same principles in mind, and instead of tending to your significant other, make sure you are investing in your own heart and spirit. You are doing the work for two and you are amazing. You need to keep your self-love beating, your personal self-support system strong, and a deep internal knowing that you are enough flowing to keep your work as a parent as light as it possibly can be. It is so important to nurture and honor you. **Stop**, and make time for this.

REFLECT

1. What or who has the power to take you off your center the most? Why? How do you handle this?

2. How do you practice personal compassion and compassion for others? Which one are you more accomplished at?

3. Does reaction have a spot at your family table? If so, outline ways to weave more response into your daily routine. How can you get yourself to **stop**? Do you need physical prompts and if so, what do those look like for you?

CEREMONIAL SUGGESTION

Write down any challenges you have faced in your life that are weighing you down or keeping you from living the life you desire. After you compile this list, add a simple line at the top that reads, "I am free from my struggles, they do not define me." Free yourself from this baggage. Once you have completed this writing exercise, find a safe and appropriate place to burn this list and release it to the universe. You will no longer have to carry the weight of your stories or your past that are impacting how you show up on a daily basis. You are free to start fresh and create a path you are proud of. Do something nurturing for yourself once this exercise has been completed.

CHAPTER 4: INCREASED AWARENESS OF PATTERNS

"Depending on what they are, our habits will either make us or break us. We become what we repeatedly do." - Sean Covey

Being aware of your patterns, habits, and the reinforcements you use as a parent is vital. If you aren't aware of what you are doing and how you are behaving, it makes it tough to lead your child in a helpful way. Awareness is akin to being conscious of your behavior and choices. When you become conscious of your thoughts, the way you speak to others and the actions you are taking on a daily basis, you are then able to determine what is serving you and what is holding you back. When you are choosing to lead with negative reinforcements, flaws, or bad habits as your go-to, then you are opening Pandora's box for potential chaos and emotional upset to ensue. If this is ringing a bell, please take a moment to **stop** and self-reflect.

FLAWS

Lean into your flaws. **Stop** is really all about examining the merit of your flaws, looking at how you have been living from a place of reaction or from a place of responding, and pausing to see the beauty in the spaces that don't feel beautiful as a parent. When you **stop**, you can then see more clearly where additional work might still be needed. Don't judge these spaces; approach them with curiosity. Flaws are part of being human, and we all have them. Having radical self-compassion for yourself up to this point will allow you to soften and see the places in your life where you might need to call in more ease. It helps you wipe the lens of judgment to start anew and perhaps have more empathy for the road you have been traveling.

Where you are struggling the most in life is where you need the most teaching, and honestly the most self-awareness. Instead of getting upset or frustrated by any self-perceived short comings or bad habits you have as a parent, look at them with a magnifying glass and figure out why these habits or patterns keep surfacing. You also might consider thanking these bad habits for all they have taught you and then do the work to release them to make room for something new to take root.

When we hold our flaws up for close examination, we can see how these habits or patterns started, and how they have or have not served us before we can properly release them. An outside support system can be invaluable, especially to help you with accountability and releasing habits that are potentially causing more harm than good.

Also, if comparing yourself to others is something you struggle with or is something that has become an unconscious habit, it is helpful to keep in mind that the success of others doesn't equate to your failure. I mention this because society in many ways brings you up to compare yourself and your experiences to what you see in the media, in magazines, or in the world around you. What you admire in the work of other parents or others in general is something you are capable of. Just because someone else is practicing or succeeding at something you strive or hope to do doesn't mean you can't do it too. You can become what you admire most. In most instances, you are your biggest limiting factor. You have to believe you are enough to be enough. In fact, I believe we all are already enough, we have simply forgotten or just don't recognize our own brilliance. It is about turning our brilliance on and not looking back unless it is to help someone else rise.

Despite your best efforts, finding balance and a state of ease can be challenging some days. The more we aim to find balance and ease in our own lives, the better able we are to show up in a healthier and more authentic state for our children and those we love. Aim to take note of where in your life you may be rushing, feeling any imbalances, or speaking in a way that is unhelpful or even hurtful and hindering progress. Try to make subtle shifts that will lift you out of these habituated patterns. This is the place where you again **stop** and take time to look within deeply.

NEGATIVE REINFORCEMENT

Negative reinforcement of your child's behavior potentially can lead to more negativity on the home front. It will in many instances have the opposite effect of the one you are likely striving for. Negative reinforcement is based on the idea that if you punish an action, it decreases the likelihood of it continuing and if you reinforce an action, it will be more likely to occur again in the future. Oftentimes negative reinforcement is accomplished by the removal of an object or event that is aversive. For example, if your child does not complete the task you have assigned to them then they lose the privilege to go out and play. The potential for losing the ability to go out and play can be a big motivator for your child to get the job done. While negative reinforcement is certainly not all bad and can be quite effective, there is an underlying negativity present as the main motivator, and I believe there is a better way to motivate others than having to constantly bargain with consequences.

This can be a tough pattern to break if you learned this

style of parenting or are currently living in this reality on a daily basis, especially if you have been for a time. I am still striving here to continually improve as a parent and don't always hit the mark I intend to. This is another moment to **stop** and reflect. This isn't a time to shame yourself for your past behavior or current parenting style, but an opportunity to start anew and consider a different way of working with your child. Every day, every minute, there is an opportunity to make a change or a shift. Let that sink in. The choice is always yours, every minute of every day.

Parenting using negative reinforcement as the primary means of delivery aims to reduce unwanted behavior, but it doesn't always offer choices or instruction on how to respond in a more appropriate manner for your child. This style of parenting can be effective, and is certainly not all bad, but it tends to be more punitive in nature. Another issue with this style of parenting is that if you do not respond immediately to your child's unwanted behavior and let too much time lapse before you take action, you essentially have been totally ineffective at delivering your message in a way that sinks in for your child. All they recognize is that they are getting in trouble, but may have lost the linking connection to the initial infraction. This essentially nullifies the whole interaction, making you less effective at delivering your message and setting appropriate boundaries in your home.

Remember, your children do not have the ability to assess situations and respond as an adult would.

Here's a common example of negative reinforcement you might experience in your home. Say you argue with your child about cleaning up their room or doing their homework. The whole goal of this style of parenting is to try and get your child to do what you want, delivered in a heightened manner, for the end goal being they clean their room or do their homework. Raising your voice will probably get their attention (negative stimulus), but how effective is it in having them keep their room clean or get their homework done on a regular basis moving forward? They may learn to clean up or do their homework to have mom or dad stop scolding them, but it ultimately can set the stage for this heightened interaction to continue on a regular basis and have the opposite effect you are hoping for. Raising your voice teaches them that in order to clean their room or do their homework, they can wait for mom or dad to get upset to get them motivated or moving. It also models this behavior for their future families because that is what they know and what has been part of their foundational structuring. This becomes an exhausting exchange and cycle, both for you and for your child, and is ultimately counterproductive. If you feel you need to communicate in a heightened manner to get your message across, this is the perfect time to **stop,** take a deep breath, self-assess, and pivot appropriately.

Positive reinforcement and leaning on the collaborative problem-solving method can be good alternatives to utilizing negative reinforcement. These approaches can help you become more effective in working with your child, and I will delve into that in more detail in a later chapter. In the meantime, moving forward, strive to have an awareness of how you respond or react to your child. Self-awareness and mindfulness of how your actions and words impact others is such an important step in growing. Choices you make can have ripple effects in a positive or negative direction, so attempt to be intentional about how you behave and interact with those around you. This is especially true with children. Think of ways to make your child's day just a little bit brighter. Seek balance and a deeper level of awareness in your every day. The more you create inner peace and awareness, the more those behaviors will be mirrored in your household. These concepts are tightly linked and will lead to a more resilient and robust family life.

SHADOW WORK

Stop any resistance you have towards owning your shadows. What do I mean by shadow? The parts of you that you don't want anyone else to see. The parts of you that hold trauma, secrets, and things that feel heavy on your heart and spirit.

We all have something. Start bringing things to the surface so you can clear them and release any hold they have on you. This doesn't mean you have to share these things with others unless you wish to or find that healing. You can do this work on your own if that serves you best and feels like the most appropriate course of action. Whether you realize it or not, those shadows have a tendency to weigh you down if you don't let them go.

Dealing with any personal wounding on your path is also something to bring into focus when working towards being a more conscious and connected parent. Many of us carry deep wounds that we hide from the world. While we become proficient at hiding the wounding that lies under the surface, the wounding is still there. It is alive, breathing, and perhaps taking a mental or physical toll on your being, whether you realize it or not. When you are carrying something that feels heavy, consider laying it down and releasing it so you aren't a prisoner of your past lived experience. Let the past live in the past, and don't continue to make it your present or your future, as this takes away from what you have to give.

I started being open to shadow work personally a few years ago, and it really started to free me as a mother and a woman. I recall a period when I was intentionally working on clearing and honoring different things from my past. I had a dream during this time where I was on an island with a wolf, and the wolf was chasing me. I initially felt fear and began to run, but then I had a moment of clarity in my dream state where I stopped running, turned, and faced the wolf. As it drew nearer, I opened my arms and embraced this wolf that was initially on the attack. The fear subsided, and I felt relief and peace.

I have moments where I can dream lucidly, and when this happens, I have made a commitment to myself that I will face down any fears that arise in my dreams instead of fleeing. This is a parallel for parenting as well. Whether things show up in your waking life or in your dreamtime, I believe they are there for a reason. Perhaps they are another opportunity to keep learning and growing. Do not flee. Instead, embrace those parts you have hidden away, so you can liberate your mind, body, and spirit.

MAKE AMENDS

I remember a few years ago I said to one of my sons independent of his brothers when we were on an outing together, "I'm sorry if I have been too hard on you at times over the years." He immediately shot back to me, "I'm sorry if I have been too hard on you too." This floored me.

Literally, jaw on the floor. This was a serious moment of reckoning for me as a parent. I couldn't believe the depth of this response from my–at the time–10 year old, and his ability to strike a place in my heart with such intensity and rawness. It was a moving exchange to say the least. I then offered this same exact apology to another one of my children, again when he was independent of his siblings, and he had the same response to me as his brother, "I'm sorry I have been too hard on you too." *Wow, wow, wow.* To have this identical response from two of my children was eye-opening, gave me deeper insight into their worlds, and more compassion for both of our journeys, from the perspective of both the parent and the child.

Both roles have challenges and take work. We need to honor one another as we work side-by-side, and recognize that it's not necessarily easy for either party all the time. There will be growing pains. Making amends is important; when mistakes are made or unhelpful words have been thrown, going back to the basics and saying, "I'm sorry," is powerful medicine. Apologizing is not a weakness, it is a strength, and it teaches your child that reconciling and making amends with others is part of creating a healthy and healing dynamic, especially at the family level.

REFLECT

1. What are your bad habits? Name them, list them, own them.

2. Is negative reinforcement something you currently use in your family? If so, how is it serving or taking away from your parenting experience?

3. Is apologizing part of your family plan? How does this show up? What does a good apology look or feel like?

PART 2

DROP

CHAPTER 5: FOLLOW THEIR LEAD & LET GO

"Keep your children wild-don't make them grow up too fast. Let them spend their days in the sunshine using their imagination. They are the change! Those wild children daydreaming in the sunshine will grow into grounded adults with minds and spirits capable of creating a better future."
- Brooke Hampton

This section is all about learning to **drop** any drama, trauma, personal history, or lived experiences that are taking away from your ability to parent from a place of living in the now. When you can **drop** these things and not allow them to take center stage in your life, it allows you to parent with more wholeness and more intentionality. Letting these things go is not about forgetting them, it is about learning to honor where you have been without letting it take away from what is right in front of you. To take this one step further, I also challenge you to **drop** what you think you know and let your child show you who they are. This is a tall order, but I believe in you and your capacity to continue to **grow**.

We have been taught we need to mold our children to fit into society to a level so restricting we often cut off their own imagination and creativity. There are basics that need to be taught so that children can appropriately engage with others and get along productively in our world. However, there should and could be much more room for freedom of expression. Kids should be allowed to daydream, spend time in deep imagination, take their shoes off and squish in the mud, run and play, and spend much more time in nature. Many of today's youth, and honestly today's adults, are quite disconnected from the natural world, which is truly a shame. Mother Nature is a powerful and gentle teacher.

There is much healing and growth that comes from spending time outdoors. Make time to connect here–it benefits both you and your child tremendously to connect with the wild.

Additionally, getting your kids hooked on nature will be something they can cherish. Teaching them to care about our beautiful Earth is vital; she can use all the support she can get. We need to remember these roots and how we are all linked. **Drop** any disconnection and get back in touch with the basics. Honor your child, and take care not to discount their daydreams and wildest creativity, perhaps theirs will spark yours.

As a family, we have prioritized getting our boys outdoors and engaged with nature as much as possible since they were little. We let our boys go barefoot, get dirty, and really live what it means to be free as a young person. Over the years, we have let them explore the world around them, climb trees, study insects and animals, be curious, and have a deep reverence for the external wilderness we have been blessed to know. In addition, we also have worked to foster the internal wilderness that stirs in us all, helping our boys to discover and explore the parts of themselves that sometimes society squishes.

A favorite memory of mine was when we were on a family trip years ago. It had been raining, and we started down a path to take a hike, but soon discovered the rain had made the path too muddy for walking on, and it was going to be tough going with four little ones. Not to be discouraged from our adventure, we found another way to play that day. We happened to be near the ocean and there were tide pools that ran along this path. What normally were dry hills had turned into towers of mud with the rain that had been falling. The boys instinctively kicked off their shoes, took their shirts off, and ran to those mud towers. There was no hesitation. It was full on mud wrestling, tower climbing, and mudslinging done the way only little boys know how–with their whole beings. They were absolutely delighted and carried on in this manner for probably an hour. My husband and I watched them and didn't redirect or tell them to stop. We let them guide their own play and immerse themselves in this experience fully. It was joyful to witness and be present for. It is a vivid memory that stands out because we didn't discourage what came naturally to them. We let them be wild and free. When they tuckered themselves out, we used the tide pools to clean them up and then all headed back to the car with huge smiles on our faces because the adventure that found us that day left a beautiful mark on all our hearts.

BOXED

What kind of world are we creating when so many are being molded into the same box? If your child doesn't seem to fit in the box, perhaps it's time to **drop** it. Let that box fall away and don't look back. It's like trying to fit a square peg in a round hole, it's just not going to happen, and if you force it, there may be undesirable lasting consequences for both you and your child. Honor their spirit and their journey. This is a period of deep imprinting for your child, so work with care, for their spirits are precious and fragile. Some friction or challenge may be appropriate to help with growth, but too much becomes counterproductive and potentially ineffective.

If a school setting seems to be a constant struggle, consider looking into other school options, if that's available. If a particular sport or activity is a battle and every time you try to have them go you receive pushback, why continue the battle? It might have been a sport you loved or have been part of your family tradition, but your child has their own sense of direction, and it might be very different from your own. Partner with them when scheduling activities and events, as it will help them blossom and create more harmony in day-to-day transitions. When your child is little, you will be the primary scheduler of all activities, but as they grow, they will want to become more involved in having a say about the details of how they spend their time and who they spend it with.

Honor this partnership and allow their voice to be heard. Work to avoid a battle that doesn't need to be waged in the first place. Parent smart here, folks. On the flip side, this isn't a license for your child to do nothing. I believe having wholesome activities, music, art, or athletics is healthy for our youth and keeps them on a path of more clarity and health as they navigate the waters of childhood. This means letting them help with what is being scheduled, it doesn't mean letting them talk you into doing nothing and playing video games instead. Wink, wink.

DRAMA

Whether you are the instigator of drama or the recipient, it is important to acknowledge that it usually doesn't feel good on either side. If you are instigating drama in life and in relationships, it might feel okay or familiar in the moment, but often afterwards there are feelings of regret. If you are the recipient, it typically doesn't feel good, appreciated, or healthy at all. Living with drama can cause feelings of hurt, be emotionally taxing, lead to feelings of guilt, and can take things to a level likely not necessary or helpful.

Work to **drop** drama from your life whenever you can. Remember you have little eyes watching you at home, so proceed with care and in a way you want reflected for your children. Unless you are taking a drama course in an academic setting, I recommend not operating from this space or in this manner with others–especially those you care about. If there are relationships in your life that seem to orbit around drama, maybe consider how these relationships are adding to or taking away from your experience and proceed accordingly, so you are better able to step into a space of health and wholeness.

TRAUMA & PERSONAL HISTORY

Trauma is a tough one. This can show up in many different forms and be very distinct for each person. Suffering deep trauma can impact you in ways that can be hard to overcome and live with. The three types of trauma are acute, chronic, and complex. Acute trauma stems from a single event, chronic from prolonged and repeated exposure (such as abuse, bullying, or domestic violence), and complex trauma involves being exposed to multiple traumatic events that tend to be more invasive in nature, such as sexual abuse. Learning to **drop** trauma can be an incredibly difficult hurdle to overcome, especially depending on the root cause.

Trauma can lead to difficulty concentrating, can impact your sleep, lead to self-destructive behavior, cause feelings of exhaustion, anxiety, and depression among other things. This is why it is so important to learn to release any hold trauma may have on your life, so you can parent from a place of freedom and peace. Releasing drama, trauma, and any difficult personal history that may be present for you likely would be best to do with the support of a licensed professional to help you navigate those waters safely and with the highest level of support.

With the intensity of what is asked in this chapter, I offer that while you do the work to **drop** things from your life that aren't helping you show up the way you want to, remember that parents like you are indeed warriors and sometimes you need to **drop** your shield, be held, and be told it's all right. Sometimes you need to cry and let go because the journey is not always an easy one. You need the very things you offer your kids daily. Don't be afraid to be held and soothed; sometimes that is the remedy and salve to continue on. Sometimes we need to return to the basics to reset. Fall into that and allow room in your life for this to be okay. There is a certain level of trauma you face personally, but also that which you encounter rearing children.

When your child is first born, you worry that they might stop breathing at night when they sleep. When they are toddlers, you worry that they might fall down the stairs, choke, or hurt themselves climbing up a bookcase. When they are elementary age you are scared that they might get run over crossing the street or riding their bike to school, and when they are teenagers that they might get into drugs, alcohol, or a car accident. There is underlying concern at every stage of the parenting process, so allow room for yourself to give love, support, and be the holder, but don't forget to be held yourself along the way.

REFLECT

1. How do you honor your child and make them feel heard and appreciated in your family?

2. What drama, trauma, or past personal history is showing up in your life and keeping you from truly being in the now with yourself and your family? Are you willing to let it go? Why or why not?

3. Do you parent from a top down approach or are you open to more partnership with your child? Is partnership in decision making an option in your family, why or why not?

CHAPTER 6: ANCESTRAL CLEARING

"When we heal ourselves, we heal our ancestors from wounds that run deep in our family. When we heal our ancestors, we heal the world from wounds that run deep in humanity." - Miriam Rose

I grew up as the oldest in my family. It was just my sister and me, and since we didn't have the easiest road cut out for us, we did a lot of bushwhacking so to speak. I learned from a young age that I was cut out to be a caretaker. My mother was not able to care for us as a typical mother would, so at age seven we went to live with our father permanently. At the time, it was not particularly customary for a father to raise two daughters on his own, so that in and of itself was an oddity.

There my father found himself, in his late thirties with two young daughters in tow. He struggled with alcohol at the time, with a smoking addiction to boot. My father had barely been able to raise himself, yet he was being asked to step into the full-time caregiver role, with little preparation, and with habits that were not ideal for being the primary caregiver. The three of us did our best to make it work though and had some grand adventures along the way. My dad has always had a heart of gold. I've worked to **drop** any parts of my childhood that feel less than because quite frankly, there is no changing it, and everything I experienced as a child has helped shape me into who I am today.

I had a lot of freedom growing up and did not suffer the helicopter parent syndrome you see today with our youth. I would often lose myself playing in the woods; building forts, climbing trees, or riding my bike up and down our dirt road for hours. I had as much freedom as I wanted–oftentimes too much! One of the things I will always be grateful to my father for is teaching me to love nature. He would take us hiking and would spend endless hours on the lake with us swimming, skiing, tubing, and really just having a great time. This is a gift I will forever cherish.

At age seven, and honestly even before that, I stepped into a mothering role that I have carried with me always. I didn't have the support I needed or the role model of a mother to help guide me on my journey, so being ever resilient, I stepped up to the plate and helped care for my father and my younger sister the best way I knew how. I actually learned how to drive a boat and a car at this age. When we would go to the bars with my dad and he would have too much to drink, it would be my responsibility to help navigate us home. At the time it was normal for me, and I usually didn't mind because it meant my sister and I got to sit at the bar and have pizza and Shirley Temples. Despite the underlying wounding here, that is still a fond memory for me. Memories are what we make of them, and I have worked hard in my life to not let my past define my future or my outlook on life. This has served me incredibly well.

Shortly after we went to live with my dad, he decided to quit drinking and smoking all together. He realized that the road he had been traveling wasn't sustainable for parenting, especially single parenting, so he successfully gave both addictions up. He tells my sister and I we saved his life. He has never picked either habit back up and thankfully enjoys a healthy life to date. He was able to **stop, drop** and begin to **grow & glow**.

One of the other pieces that was challenging is that my father worked out of town and so would travel and be gone during the week. He was home only on the weekends for a large portion of my childhood, so my sister and I would stay with different families or couples in his absence.

Some of these experiences were great and some not so great. Being shuffled around and not having a true sense of home and foundation was tough. The lack of consistency was also at times hard. I've had to **drop** this foundational experience;

not forget it, but not carry it with me so it won't weigh me down.

My father dated off and on during my childhood and we were exposed to some kind women who did step in to temporarily fill the mother role; it was a gift to not go the whole journey alone, and I did gather some pearls along the way that I will be forever grateful for. It was always particularly crushing for me when the relationships ended, as this was a tender spot for me. When I was fifteen, my father met a woman who ended up sticking around, and she became the constant mother figure I had always craved. I had never before experienced this kind of consistency. I was beyond grateful she knew how to fill this void and provide structure and rhythm to our small family unit. She was fun, charismatic, organized, an amazing cook, kind, and a blessed storyteller. She had a way of pulling you in and charming you with her endless and timeless personality. It was particularly crushing to lose her so unexpectedly in 2016.

Sometimes when I look back on my childhood, I wish I had had two parents to read me bedtime stories, come to all my sporting events, and do the things that a "normal" family would have done. However, I really believe that my experiences have made me who I am today. I have a rich understanding and empathy for others facing the same struggles. I have a deep desire to give parents more tools so they can give their children a brighter experience and learn to nurture themselves in the process. I also feel especially grateful that my husband and I can give our boys what I did not receive as a child. I am closing this gap and creating a new story moving forward. This is the perfect opportunity to **drop** any stories that are currently propelling you forward in a way that is not truly serving you or your children. We all come from different walks and different pasts, but what we do today is what matters most. Have a clear vision of how to manifest the life you are envisioning, and don't let any historical familial challenges or past struggles define who you are now or how you are choosing to parent and live your life.

Some say that we choose this lifetime before we incarnate, and if that is the case, then you chose this path. *Wow*! For me, when I think about it in those terms, it makes me realize that this is the work I came here to do. It puts things in a whole new perspective. As my husband often lovingly reminds me, this isn't a dress rehearsal; I better get it in gear and get it right the first time around. This also makes me laugh on days it feels especially challenging raising my children, and I sometimes pause and think to myself, *I chose this path? Really?!* I am joking here, and I wouldn't trade being a mother for anything, but my goodness, there are days motherhood pushes you to your outer limits. Children have a way of pushing every button you never knew you had and then pulling you back in with a love that is so fierce and so complete that you just can't get enough. It is that rollercoaster of emotions that is the ultimate training ground for learning how to make contact with your conscious self. This is the perfect opportunity to step into being a more conscious and grounded parent amid the fluctuations.

HONOR YOUR ROOTS

Look for ways to connect to your ancestors. Read books, connect with other family members who may know your family's history, ask your parents and grandparents to share with you stories and ways of life when they were young. These are such rich means of connecting, honoring your heritage, and remembering where your roots lie. If you do not know your family's history, opt for current methods of looking at your DNA to see where you come from. This information is humbling and also exciting to explore. There is much available in the world today to assist with digging deeper and learning more related to your lineage. Knowing what makes you *you* is part of the journey, and this history should not be forgotten. Be intentional in learning about your origins, and don't forget to share your stories with the next generation. Share this rich information with your kids and help them understand who they are in a deeper way. If you are unclear about your family history, then now is the perfect time to have this new generation start with you. Create beautiful traditions in your own family that your children can then pass on to their young.

In the same vein as honoring your roots, be sure to unravel your travel. What does this mean? It means letting go of any muck or ancestral baggage you might have carried up to today.

Unravel the bits and pieces of you that might feel wound tight and possibly cutting off your vitality and ability to truly thrive. Let what has or hasn't happened to you up to now simply fall away. It is not about forgetting or minimizing the road you've been asked to travel, but it is also not about letting the travel be what defines you today. We are ever-changing creatures that are capable of astounding beauty, tremendous growth, and great potential. Don't forget to remind yourself of this. It can be easy to forget when you are knee-deep in child rearing responsibilities and have little ones tugging at you around the clock.

Additionally, honor traditions that may be losing footing as we catapult into the future. While we are living in an exciting and ever-changing time, it is grounding to look back and pull from some of the more simplistic ways of existing. One idea worth exploring is the intentional act of transitioning in a slower way, such as our ancestors did. Be more methodical about how you transition from one activity to the next, and infuse mindfulness and ease into your daily life. Instead of rushing, **stop** and breathe, and know that the next item on your list will be waiting whether you are flying around or making the choice to touch down softly. I will go into further depth about transitioning intentionally in a later chapter but wanted to plant the seed here to get you thinking about what that might look like. Find a pace that may be more in-step with days gone by, even if it's only one day a week. See if this creates more balance and happiness in how you approach your day and your parenting style. Honor your ancestors. Trace your roots. Find more ease in your everyday.

Mantras can help provide inner power and help you feel strong as you work to let go of what does not serve or is no longer necessary in your life. A simple mantra or prayer I use almost daily is: *May my ancestral lineage be clean, clear, and made whole.* I put energy here to seal the cracks in my family tree, so that my children do not have to walk the same path I did. This feels important to me, so I tend it and keep awareness here. If this resonates with you, consider using this mantra because it matters, especially if there are fractures in your family tree of origin. If there are not any fractures and you've come from a strong and healthy family tree, you might use a mantra such as: *May my ancestral lineage continue to be blessed, whole, and healthy.* This helps seed the continuation of what is going well within your family structure and also helps you remember your consciousness here of what you want to maintain. The second mantra offered is more of a maintenance protocol.

REFLECT

1. Do you know your ancestral history? Have you talked with elders in your family about your family of origin? If this knowledge isn't available, have you done a DNA test to learn more? Take some time to explore this.

2. How does your ancestral knowledge impact your parenting style? Are there traditions you honor annually? If not, make time to come up with meaningful traditions you want to start in your own family that your children can then carry with them as they grow. List at least two to get the ball rolling.

3. Is there any ancestral wounding that still needs to be unpacked? Any skeletons in the closet that need to be released that will help you be a more fluid and grounded parent? Make time to dance with these shadows and then journal or do work to help let them go so these wounds do not pass to the next generation. Never be afraid to ask for professional help if needed.

PART 3

GROW

Chapter 7: Hormones

"To control your hormones is to control your life." - Barry Sears

Hormonal balance is an issue that doesn't seem to take the spotlight as much as it should with child rearing. This is a major area to learn more about in order to **grow** as a parent. When hormones are properly functioning, life may seem to tick by with ease, but when things are off-kilter it can permeate every part of your day in a way that might not be in alignment with the true you.

Hormones are chemicals mainly from glands that send out signals to your organs, muscles, tissues, and skin via the blood, and tell your body what to do and when to do it. This is known as the endocrine system; there actually have been over 50 different hormones identified in the human body, which is truly remarkable.

Hormones are vital to life, longevity, and health. Hormones work to regulate the sleep-wake cycle, your metabolism, growth and development, sexual function, homeostasis (internal balance), mood, and reproduction. These are all incredibly important functions in life, so it is paramount that your body is working in alignment, and that hormonal balance is intact physiologically so you can function as you are meant to (*Hormonal imbalance*, 2021.).

SLEEP

After childbirth, hormones can get out of sync for women, related to changes in sex hormones. Both men and women can suffer issues with their hormone levels, especially related to sleep deprivation. Sleep alterations and deprivation can lead to abnormal levels of cortisol. Cortisol is a key hormone linked to your metabolism that works to suppress inflammation and regulate your body's stress response and blood sugar.

Abnormal cortisol levels can wreak havoc on your internal system. "Almost all tissues in your body have glucocorticoid receptors. Because of this, cortisol can affect nearly every organ system in your body," (*Hormonal imbalance*, 2021). Specifically, the respiratory system, cardiovascular system, immune system, nervous system, musculoskeletal system, integumentary system (which includes skin, glands, nerves, nails, and hair), and reproductive systems. This list is pretty comprehensive and shows just how important it is to have a properly functioning hormonal system. This highlights one of the reasons why you feel so crummy the day after inadequate sleep. It taxes your body on just about every level.

Sleep deprivation not only impacts hormones, but is also associated with Type 2 diabetes, obesity, hypertension, heart disease, mood disorders, and decreased immune function (*Sleep and disease risk*, 2022). During sleep is when our body repairs itself and works through problems of the day. While you can't always get the rest you need as a parent, it is paramount that you prioritize doing your best to get the most sleep you can. I remember when my boys were first born and my doctor recommended, "nap when your kids nap during the day." This was sage advice, and advice worth passing on because it helps work as a buffer for those nights that your little one is up and not letting you get a solid stretch of sleep.

Learning about hormonal imbalance is particularly thought-provoking as it gives us insight into internal damages happening when sleep is not occurring the way it's supposed to. Hormones are definitely impacted, but so is our DNA and our organs. We are a complex interconnected network, so it is not altogether surprising that damage is occurring when we don't have the ability or time to prioritize sleep, as this is our body's time to repair itself. When we are raising children, especially right after they are born but continuing for years afterwards, sleep is often disturbed, and parents are required to sleep on a partial night regimen. Sleep plays an integral role in our health, mood, aging, immunity, and ability to function on a daily basis. It is also amazing how adaptable our bodies are and what they put up with over the years. If sleep is currently a concern in your life, try to find ways to make time to get more z's. Your body, your mind, and your children will thank you.

HPA AXIS DYSFUNCTION

Hypothalamic-Pituitary-Adrenal axis dysfunction is a bit of a mouthful, but a process I want to discuss because it is something I personally struggled with for a time as a mother, and I suspect there are parents out there who may be struggling with this as well but may not have an awareness or knowledge about what it is. HPA dysfunction has been called adrenal fatigue and is a bit of a controversial term not always widely accepted by mainstream medicine.

The thought behind HPA dysfunction is that the adrenal hormones are not functioning properly, and chronic stress, postpartum, medications, and other conditions may cause this. Most commonly, the adrenals are not producing enough cortisol to keep up with demand due to chronic stress. The pathophysiology behind this is complex, involving the HPA axis and the tissue systems it impacts. The controversy is in part due to lab value often showing normal levels. There can be subtle abnormalities in hormone levels, feedback mechanisms, and tissue sensitivity. To complicate this even more, the sympathetic nervous system (the fight or flight system) is triggered by stress and creates more issues.

When you are parenting little ones, you have to be on non-stop. This in and of itself is exhausting and often is combined with less than ideal sleep, which can be a breeding ground for the body to start to dysregulate. With so much on my plate with four kids, I finally started to feel the effects of being under intense daily demands and was feeling pretty drained and fatigued on a regular basis. This was the personal catalyst for me reaching out to my health care professional to figure out the root of the problem. After an appropriate evaluation and doing hormonal testing, I learned there were multiple interventions to improve my symptoms. I then chose natural supplements to boost my system and made some lifestyle modifications to help support me at a more optimal level. This experience helped me **grow**, made a huge difference in my daily life as a mother, and improved my health and ability to rally and show up for my children.

The group Simply Psychology shared this list of signs and

symptoms of HPA, which includes, but is not limited to:

- Feeling irritable
- Frequent illnesses
- Difficulty coping with stress
- Feeling unexplainable tiredness
- Feeling overwhelmed
- Experiencing an exaggerated response to stress

These symptoms can be difficult to deal with, but on a positive note, one of the most effective ways to treat symptoms of HPA is by making lifestyle changes to really bolster your system. More specifically,

1. Exercise regularly and include both cardio and resistance training.
2. Increase protein intake at breakfast to reset cortisol function and decrease blood sugar.
3. Decrease sugar in your diet and eliminate added sugars.
4. Practice stress management and utilize meditation and breath work.
5. Avoid or limit alcohol and caffeine.
6. Get quality sleep as often as is possible.

Additional avenues or resources to explore to help alleviate hormonal symptoms or imbalance are Ayurveda, holistic coach or naturopath, health care professional, mind or body alignment practices, meditation, and yoga.

WARNING SIGNS OF GENERALIZED HORMONAL IMBALANCE

Pregnancy and postpartum cause more pronounced fluctuation in hormones than normal, as do puberty, menopause, stress, and medication use. Hormone disturbances may be minor, or due to a serious underlying disorder. Be mindful of signs and symptoms that could indicate a problem.

Signs and symptoms of hormonal imbalance (these symptoms also can be caused by other conditions as well) for women according to the Cleveland Clinic (2021) include, but are not limited to:

- Mood swings
- Fatigue
- Infertility
- Irregular periods
- Vaginal dryness
- Hirsutism (excess body hair)
- Dry, coarse skin and hair
- Irregular body fat distribution
- Constipation
- Depression and anxiety

- Extreme thirst and frequent urination
- Acne
- Inability to tolerate cold or hot temperatures
- Slow or rapid heartbeat
- Numbness and tingling in your hands

FOR MEN:

- Erectile dysfunction
- Loss of muscle mass
- Gynecomastia (enlarged breast tissue)
- Loss of desire for sex
- Decrease or loss of body hair

You know your symptoms and physical self best and know if something is off. If troubling feelings or physical abnormalities are presenting, you absolutely should reach out to a health care professional to help you come back into alignment. Again, release any self-judgement here, there are many, many others who find themselves struggling with hormonal fluxes that are not serving them, their bodies, or their families. Knowing your personal baseline is helpful in identifying if there is an issue present or not. Practice self-compassion and create spaciousness for yourself to receive support if it is needed. This is a major area to allow outside expertise into your life, which can be beneficial to help you realign and come back home to yourself.

PREVENTION

If you are curious about ways to prevent hormonal imbalances, know that it will require mindfulness and some work on your part. This work can include managing your stress, regular exercise, eating a healthy diet, maintaining a healthy weight, getting quality sleep, quitting smoking (if you smoke), and managing any chronic health conditions if they exist. These prevention strategies can work to keep your delicate chemistry functioning at an optimal level. If, despite your best efforts, your hormonal system still feels off, reach out for additional support and recommendations. This is especially applicable for women during pregnancy, and up to five years after the birth of each child for both men and women. This is the time when you are sleeping the least and asked the most of daily, so it's important to keep tabs on yourself during this time frame (and possibly beyond, depending on your circumstances, number of children, and home or work environment).

KIDS & HORMONES

Not only do you have to consider your own and possibly your partners hormonal fluxes, but you also have to factor in your child's ever changing hormonal situation as well. Puberty for boys begins between the ages of nine and fourteen and for girls between eight and thirteen, although there are always outliers on either side of those ages to keep in mind. Girls have estrogen and progesterone cycling through their bodies, while boys have testosterone. With puberty can come moodiness, conflict with parents, and emotional outbursts. It can be easy to forget as a parent that your child is undergoing many changes that aren't visible to the eye. Compassion is called for here, especially when your child is unpredictable or acting out in ways that aren't "normal."

If your child's behavior seems severe, you should be consulting a health care provider for additional support or intervention. Most children make it through puberty intact and healthy; you just have to be there to support them in whatever arises. Be available for your children if they need to or want to talk. I find bedtime pillow talk is one of the best times to check in with your child about how things are going for them personally, socially, or otherwise. Taking time to check in daily with your child at any age about their day is encouraged. This is a great way to bond and gain trust with your child so you can be a safe place for them to land if they need.

Additionally, I am a huge fan of sleep for children. Sleep is where our bodies rest and repair cellularly. It also is the time when your child's brain releases the growth hormone (GH). GH is responsible for development and growth and ensures that your child is growing at a normal pace. It also is involved in the regulation of proteins, fats, carbohydrates, and calcium in children and adults. When sleep deprivation occurs, it suppresses the release of the growth hormone. Many people aren't aware of this, so it's something noteworthy for sure to tuck away in your parenting database.

With screen time an ever-persistent issue to combat, it's worth having a routine for bedtime, including turning screens off at least an hour (ideally more than an hour) before bedtime so the brain can start preparing to rest and slow down. According to the CDC, toddlers (one to two years old) should aim for 11 to 14 hours of sleep every day (24 hour time frame); preschool age (three to five years old) need 10 to 13 hours of sleep daily; school age (six to twelve years old) optimally would get 9 to 11 hours every day; and teenagers (thirteen to eighteen years old) should sleep 8 to 10 hours daily.

The hormonal system is indeed complex and can be confusing to fully understand and navigate. What I am encouraging you to do as a parent is to let any self-judgment or feelings of being less than fall away if you have been struggling to rally or show up the way you want to be. There may be underlying causes at work, and with some personal investigation and assistance from licensed professionals, you very well may be able to correct any imbalance that may be present. You also might be doing just fine and therefore not resonate with this, but I have found that many parents struggle with lack of sleep and the big asks of them personally when they are raising their family. Do your own research–don't just stop here–and dive deeper into the hormonal system if this is something you feel a connection to or determine might be relevant to your current situation as a mother or father.

REFLECT

1. Do you think hormonal imbalance has played a role in your parenting journey to date? If the answer is *yes*, how might this be affecting you and your family?

2. What have you noticed with your child(ren) related to hormonal changes? Do you currently have awareness about hormonal changes being part of their journey when they act out or have struggles? Or is this the first time you are pausing to consider this?

3. What changes in your lifestyle would help better support you and your hormonal system? Spend time journaling or thinking about ways to bolster your system to benefit you at the most optimal level as a parent.

Chapter 8: Mindfulness

"Quiet the mind and the soul will speak." - Ma Jaya Sati Bhagavati

Practicing mindfulness in your life as you parent will support and uplift you. Meditation, slowing your transitions, leaning on Ayurvedic principles, and tapping into your spirituality all can work to provide an internal and external foundation that will help you operate from a solid base and will help you continue to **grow**. Meditation has increasingly taken the forefront these days. This is exciting and encouraging news for humanity–it means we are waking up. Having a solid daily practice will change your life for the better. Not only will it improve your life, but ultimately those around you will feel the shift and will also benefit from you being able to center your energy in a more intentional way. Turning inward and finding stillness and quiet on a daily basis can invite so much peace and harmony into your life. Carve out time to reflect, to invite new ideas, to practice gratitude and to think loving thoughts about yourself and others to bring deep inner peace. Inner peace will then translate into being a happier parent.

Meditation is a grounding ritual. It is through silence and connecting with yourself and divine energy that the mind begins to calm. Room for personal expansion begins to take root, as well as a feeling of interconnectedness to the world around you and to your child. It is through the process of getting quiet that you really begin to hear and see more clearly in life. According to the Mayo Clinic (2022), meditation can offer many emotional and physical benefits which include: "gaining a new perspective on stressful situations, building skills to manage your stress, increasing self-awareness, focusing on the present, reducing negative emotions, increasing imagination and creativity, increasing patience and tolerance, lowering resting heart rate, lowering resting blood pressure, and improving sleep quality." Who couldn't use more of these benefits in their life? Especially parents, who work tirelessly, day in and day out.

There are many different types of meditations you can draw from, and even trying on a new practice if you have one already established can be beneficial, stimulating, and helpful in keeping your practice evolving. To name a few, there is:

- **Guided meditation**: visualization and guided imagery led by another.
- **Mantra meditation**: the practice of repeating a word or simple phrase to prevent your mind from wandering.
- **Mindfulness meditation**: practicing living and being in the present moment.
- **Tai Chi**: deep breathing combined with martial arts that keeps the mind-body in balance.

All of these options listed can work to improve your lifestyle along with your parenting path; it is about finding what resonates and fits your personality best. There is not necessarily a one-size-fits-all here. There are also many meditation apps, such as Headspace or Calm that can be helpful in carving time out for yourself on a daily basis.

A couple of other important pieces to mention is that meditation does not have to only be performed sitting still in a quiet space. If you are not keen on sitting still daily, no problem. Meditation does not have to be performed sitting cross legged with incense burning while wearing wool socks (although these can be fun additions). Walking meditation, yoga, or qigong can be ways to tap into this head and heart space, honor your way of finding a reset, and remember your conscious center. You also can draw on mindfulness meditation anywhere, anytime. It can be driving in your car, working in the office, or in between dropping your child off for activities. All that is required is your attention, your intention, and mindfulness. It is that simple. I've found the more I practice and remember, the more I want to continue and stay disciplined. It makes a difference, it matters, and it helps me immensely as a parent and as an individual.

I'd also like to drive home the importance of breath work. Breathing and breath work are key components of both a solid meditation practice and just being alive. I have spent years practicing hot yoga, where there is encouragement of breathing in and out through the nose (ujjayi pranayama). Engaging with breathing in this fashion helps calm the nervous system and the mind. In addition, it can lower the heart rate and decrease blood pressure, so it also works to help your mind and body feel more at ease.

Working to extend the inhale and exhale will help improve your lung capacity and will work to kick your parasympathetic nervous system into gear, which is responsible for relaxing your body after periods of stress or danger. It is known as the "rest and digest" part of your nervous system. Many parents and caregivers often are functioning with the sympathetic nervous system taking charge, which is responsible for "fight-or-flight" responses and is much more taxing on your system, especially when this is the primary state you are operating from the majority of the time. When you are functioning in a constant state of stress as a parent, it eventually will lead to burn out. Learning to operate and work in an intentional way will help you strike a balance which will benefit you immensely.

Lastly, an example of how you can call on breath in a mindful way is to utilize "box breathing," also known as 4444 breathing, which is a form of yogic deep breathing. I really appreciate this breathing technique because it is easy to remember. The Cleveland Clinic (2021) notes that this technique is actually used by the United States Navy SEALs, as well as people of all walks of life trying to ease tension and stress in their daily lives. To begin this breath work, first breathe out slowly, releasing all the air in your lungs. Next, inhale through your nose for four seconds. Hold this breath for four seconds. Then, exhale for four seconds and hold for four seconds. Repeat for several rounds.

The more you practice, the longer you might be able to inhale and exhale, to slow and soothe the mind. This simple practice can be a powerful stress reliever. Ideally you would be sitting in a comfortable, supported position, but really you could practice this anywhere, anytime you need it. If you forget to **stop** and breathe during the day (which is a common experience for most people, especially parents), try this when you are lying in bed at night and use it to help you unwind and calm your system before sleep. **Stop** and breathe to **drop** the tension.

It takes effort to **stop** the doing and be intentional about receiving in a way that is not busy or loud. In silence you begin to see your whole self, not just the fragmented version that is usually running from one task to the next. It is beautiful to witness yourself in this light. When you become intentional about using a meditative practice in your life, things will shift in a lovely way. If the idea of meditation itself does not appeal, even sitting in silence or using kind mantras for focus, such as "so, hum" (which means "I am that" or "Om, shanti, shanti, shanti" (which is powerful invocation for peace) can be powerful. If you combine meditation with nature, your experience will be magnified. The natural world is a powerful gateway to understanding how calming silence and inner stillness can be. Practice going within, embracing solitude, and clearing your mind.

So many things in our lives pull us away from our natural state of just being; we are inundated with a million to-do's and forget how to just be. In allowing stillness into your life, you create a space to really get to know yourself and who you are as a parent. In this place of quiet allowance, you can tap into a sacred space of stillness. It is in this stillness that peace begins to grow. The more you practice stillness, the more your mind and body will want to return to the sensation of serenity. When you find peace within, you can begin to spread that peace in our world. A lovely ripple effect will begin to take place in your life. When you are at peace, all of those you come into contact with will feel the peace and the energy you emit.

You might be thinking, *well that sounds nice, but I don't have time to find serenity in my day*. I would offer that it truly can take two minutes of focused attention and quiet to start tapping into that place inside. Perhaps you can find this time before the hustle and bustle starts in the morning (that's personally my favorite time of day to practice), when you are driving in the car to or from a commitment, or at night before you settle in. Wherever you can carve some time out in your day for you—your mind, body, and spirit will thank you. If you have more time to set aside for this personal journey of finding stillness, then that will only magnify the beautiful effects. See what a difference it can make in your life, assisting in more mindful parenting.

In our home, my children know that they have an open invitation to join me on the mat for morning meditations if they wish. This is not mandatory or forced, it is on their terms, and depends on how they are feeling any given day. I do have some guidelines they are aware of, which is to respect the space and keep it quiet. If they cannot respect these requests, then they are re-directed to find something else to do while I finish my meditation. It is amazing to witness them come and go from the mat, as well as to see who might show up to join me for this quiet time. It brings me joy to see their interest in meditation and my hope is that it will plant seeds of goodness for them as they continue to grow into adulthood.

A typical session for me begins with lighting a candle. As I do this, I say a silent prayer, *let there be more light in the world.* This simple thought in my mind is rippling through the universe, touching every beings heart. I have my green tea made and bring that into my morning ceremony as well, as this is a form of simple nourishment and joy for me. I then sit and have a bowl ready that contains crystals and sage. I turn on my infrared heater that is situated in front of me to bring a little heat and clarity to my session. Once these steps are completed, I then come into a crisscross seat, reach for my sage, and use the flame from the candle to ignite the end.

Once lit, I use this sacred herb to cleanse my energy field. It is a physical way to cleanse from root to crown and refresh any energy that is not serving me in the most beautiful way. Having an energy hygiene practice is incredibly beneficial and honors your own sacredness. As parents, we give so much of our energy away throughout the day. This can be a tremendous way to give to yourself and refresh your system, so you can then better serve those around you who are in need of your care.

Finally, I draw a card from my meditation deck for a daily inspirational message. It always amazes me how spot on these cards that show up are, depending on current life circumstances. In fact, the synchronicity never ceases to amaze me. It is a way to keep my practice feeling fresh and invite in a little outside support. After all of these steps are completed, I then go into silent meditation and prayer, anywhere from 5 to 45 minutes depending on what my time that day will allow. Additionally, at times I use guided mediation to infuse outside perspective.

Any time spent in meditation makes a difference, even if it's brief. I work to not take this sacred time for granted and remember to give thanks and honor this part of my life that means so much to me. Finally, remember to not get complacent in whatever practice you choose. Keep stoking the fire and it will in turn keep you **growing** and **glowing** from root to crown.

TRANSITIONS

One thing I have learned over the years since starting a family is the need to slow down. To make your transitions from one activity to the next slower and to not be in such a perpetual race all day long. This is a major area to **grow** as a parent if you are open to trying it out. Slowing down creates more ease and clarity and makes space for more peace to land in your daily life.

Being intentional and slowing down also teaches you not to rush your life away or jump into situations that perhaps could have used a little more thought and mindfulness. The more you rush from one thing to the next, the more stress you likely will feel. Sometimes you need to pause and let life come to you a bit.

While this might sound like a luxury to a busy parent, it is really not. It's an intentional choice. You always have the power to choose how to live and how to be. Even when you are running late for example, you have the choice to breathe and not operate from a state of panic and tension. If you are already running late, where is the win in being late and being stressed on top of it? That stress is what keeps your fight or flight nervous system stimulated! Instead, practice self-compassion, breathe, and know that you are doing the best you can. You aren't going to nail it every day. Give yourself a hug and cut yourself a break; some days that's the best prescription and perhaps the most sensible solution to the places that feel squeezed or rushed in your life.

The practice of being intentional with transitioning as a parent has been a hard lesson for me to learn, but I am finally getting the hang of it and actually really loving the shift in my life. For years, I was running from one thing to the next and not allowing room for more softness, intentionality, and grace to show up. This is something I have had to learn and practice over and over to finally see the work start to blossom. I feel more spaciousness, and I feel happier and more supported living from this conscious place. It is possible to slow down, and it is possible to make the shift no matter how busy or constricted you feel as a parent.

While we are on the topic of being more intentional with transitioning, consider teaching your child how to transition with more ease as well. Offering a five to ten minute warning before switching to another activity allows your child a few minutes to mentally prepare, instead of having their activity abruptly cut short. This can greatly improve their ability to switch gears without as much pushback. It also helps them to feel more in step with your plans as you continue with your day. This is definitely a seed worth planting with your child.

Here is a real-life example of transitions: you are in your car and you are driving the speed limit in town, while the vehicle next to you is speeding and weaving in and out of traffic, rushing to get wherever it is they are headed. How often do you then both end up sitting next to one another again at the next traffic light? All that energy expended with no gain. Use this metaphor in your parenting life. You can choose to rush, stress, and operate in a heightened manner, or you can choose to go with the flow, **grow**, find more gentility and poise, and likely end up at the same end spot. Again, the choice and remembrance of how to transition is always yours.

In the spirit of weaving a little magic into this, I want to share another personal practice of mine that has helped me shift my perspective and my reality in a positive direction, especially when I have moments of feeling rushed or behind schedule. One of my favorite active practices is to thank what is before me. Say I am driving, and I hit a string of green lights; I say, "thank you." If I am driving and hit a red light or stop sign, I also say, "thank you."

I give thanks either direction, because in one way I was allowed to stay in the flow and in the other, I was asked to stop. Maybe I had to stop because it kept me from something that wasn't meant for me. I give thanks because I know I am always where I am meant to be, whether it feels ideal or not. I share this because how many things happen every day that feel routine, but actually are teaching you deep lessons? Life in and of itself is a miraculous teaching and learning ground.

Really dig in and start to notice. Face what is in front of you with more ease, gratitude, and with the knowledge there is more timelessness than there are hands on a clock.

AYURVEDA

Ayurveda is a natural practice of medicine that originated more than 3,000 years ago. It is a traditional medical system of

India, which has three categories of fundamental regulatory principles about the mind, body, and behavior. The world is comprised of five elements, which are fire, earth, air, water, and space. From the combination of these five elements, three life energies emerge: vata, pitta, and kapha. These three life energies are known as doshas. I will very briefly describe these doshas so you can have a better understanding of what they encompass and where you might land among them because the more you know about yourself, the better you can then navigate life as a parent and a person. Understanding and familiarizing yourself with your primary dosha will help you get a clearer picture of your natural strengths and any areas where you may need more support or mindfulness. Additionally, having a baseline knowledge of your dosha will allow you to then start bringing your life into more balance–specifically your mind, body, spirit, and environment–and will allow you to enhance your well-being on all levels.

Think of your dosha as your internal blueprint, or a kind of map for deeper understanding of your personal constitution, habits, physical make-up, and your tendencies. You likely will find one dosha that fits best but will likely also resonate with the other two at some level. They are fascinating and usually quite accurate. When you find the dosha that fits you, remember to carry threads from all three, because this again helps there to be more balance in your system, especially if you lean heavily towards one and not the other two.

PITTA (FIRE & WATER)

People who resonate as being pitta dominant tend to have characteristics that align with having an athletic physique. They tend to be fierier in nature and love to win. They are natural born leaders, ambitious, and passionate. They exude strength and have a tendency to be perfectionists.

Pitta dominant people are never cold, and their hands and feet stay warm. There is a tendency for deep sleeping, and they are prone to vivid dreams. They have a strong metabolism and good appetite. Food wise, they prefer cold drinks, and enjoy both sweet and bitter foods best. Those with the combination of fire and water are known to be "hot, light, sharp, oily, liquid, and mobile," explains Medical News Today (Cronkleton, 2022), a health information platform. Summer is the season associated with this dosha, as it is hot and sunny.

KAPHA (EARTH & WATER)

Kapha dominant folks like to move at a slower pace. They are thoughtful, patient, and have a tendency to operate with high intelligence, care, and tenacity. Their physical constitution tends to be heavier, with thick bone structure and a slower metabolism. Eating brings this dosha great pleasure. Strength and endurance come naturally to those with this dosha. They also are loyal and reliable. Stubbornness and lethargy might be present.

Finding inner tranquility, harmony, and peace, as well as being compassionate and loving are also of high importance for those who are kapha dominant. They sweat easily and are more prone to oily skin. However, the skin tends to be smooth and lustrous. According to Medical News Today, the combination of earth and water, which make up this dosha, can be "described as stable, heavy, slow, cold, and soft," (Cronkleton, 2022). Spring is the season associated with the kapha dosha, a time of exiting hibernation.

VATA (AIR & SPACE)

Those who are vata dominant are communicative, enthusiastic, kind-hearted, and full of ideas. They are quick learners and excellent at multitasking. There is a tendency to spread themselves thin and become easily distracted, despite their enthusiastic nature. They can be sensitive and dynamic in personality. Physically they are highly active, tend to be leaner in stature, have a delicate bone structure, and can suffer from cold hands and feet. Additionally, they are more prone to dry skin and hair. There can be more sensitivity to cold weather and difficulty with circulation and joints as well, Medical News Today (Cronkleton,

2022) says. The combination of air and space, which make up this dosha is linked to, "change, mobility, and movement." Autumn is known as the season for the vata dosha.

I personally lean more vata dominant. With this knowledge and understanding I can see where my strengths lie, and inversely I can see where I am more prone to have challenges or need to put in more work to strike a balance. This allows me to have a deeper awareness of how to live, and of the choices I make, whether it be the environment to live in to support my system, dietary decisions, supplements, activity level needs, etc. During the winter months for example, my hands and feet are always cold, so I am mindful to wear socks or slippers and work to drink warm liquids throughout the day to help warm my internal system. I also have skin that is prone to getting dry once the weather shifts to cold, so I make sure to use organic oils or lotions to help coat, protect, and nourish my skin during this time of the year.

Proper dietary and lifestyle habits linked to your dosha can help support you on your journey once you have a clearer picture of who you are and how you operate, especially if you are out of alignment here. I recommend working with an Ayurvedic practitioner or doing your own research if your interest has been piqued, as what I have offered is just barely scratching the surface. There are many layers to this ancient medical system and much wisdom that can help you come into incredible holistic alignment if you are open to it.

I personally appreciate what an Ayurvedic approach to life can offer; what I love the most is that it takes into account a person's mind, body, spirit, and environment. Where we often drop the ball in western medicine, is the tendency to look at the presenting complaint or ailment and then focus on treating that solely. Western medicine is much more singularly focused rather than holistic, and this is unfortunate. I believe to achieve full health you can't leave out the other parts and I believe the same is true in parenting. To have true health and happiness in parenting, you must nurture your mind, body, spirit, and environment because if you are only tending to one or two of these things, you aren't going to maximize your experience, much less live with as much joy or mindfulness.

For example, you might spend a lot of time working or exercising at the gym. These are both great and will support you on your journey, but though you are ticking the boxes of mind and body, you are then neglecting to spend time tending to spirit and environment. This will have an impact at some point because there is a disconnect happening. You might not be able to honor all four of these every day but try to connect with them as often as possible because they matter, and they will make a difference in your life.

It may feel overwhelming to approach mind, body, spirit, and environment daily, but it can be remarkably simple. An example of how I weave these four into my daily life is to start my day with meditation. I tend to my spirit, ground myself, and feel a connection to the greater whole of humanity and beyond, as well as the role I am playing here in this life. My husband and I then walk our youngest son to school (our older ones have progressed to riding the bus; I miss being able to walk them these days!) and this allows me to feel connected to our natural world, tending to environment. I am always in awe of the trees, the beautiful sky, and the creatures that live in our neighborhood. This is a time for remembrance of how grateful I am for breathing fresh air and getting to live in such a beautiful place.

I also try to make time daily for movement of my body by hiking, doing yoga, or hitting the gym, because this keeps my system in check, makes me feel better, and allows for me to show up as a solid parent when I am with my kids. Finally, I tend to my mind with work, reading, writing, and all the mental gymnastics of scheduling four children, my husband, and myself. During all of this work, I try to imbue mindfulness into all four of these categories to stay in balance and find my center.

You might realize you are already ticking all of the boxes (meaning you already are regularly tending to your mind, body, spirit, and environment) and didn't even realize it. If that's the case, then well done you!

There are many different ways to nurture your mind, body, spirit, and environment. It doesn't and won't look the same for everybody. Nurturing the mind for instance could also be meditation or other activities that calm the mind, not just activities that stimulate or light up the mind. Tending to your body doesn't have to be physical, it can also be receiving self-care in the form of massage, acupuncture, or the like. Caring for your spirit can be whatever brings you peace and ease in your life, whether that be personal or part of a community. Though nurturing your environment can be spending time in nature and remembering your connection there, it also can encompass your home environment and how you structure that to support you at an optimal level.

Think broad here, don't have a limited mindset, and remember to not lose touch with any parts of you, because they all matter.

HEART CENTERED PARENTING MODEL

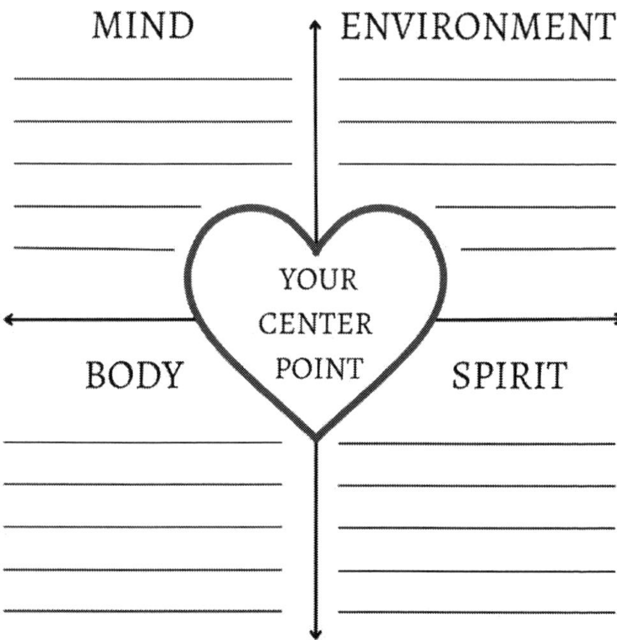

Developed by Holly Swenson

Let's break down and make sense of this image. Here, you see a drawing of four compartments and a heart in the center. The heart is your center point. It is you in the now, and you should work to hold your own and maintain your center no matter what is happening in your life. Lead from your heart space. This takes practice, loyalty to the cause, and a certain level of discipline as a parent.

Compartment 1) **Mind**: How are you honoring and tending to your mind?

Compartment 2) **Body**: How are you honoring and tending to your body?

Compartment 3) **Spirit**: How are you honoring and tending to your spirit?

Compartment 4) **Environment**: How are you honoring and tending to your environment (either your home environment or connecting to the natural environment around you)?

Ideally, you want to learn to stay in the center of this model. This is the zero point, your mid-line, optimum balance of all four quadrants, the ultimate center of health, success, joy, and more grounded and conscious parenting. The arrows that extend outside of the heart represent the work you are bringing out into the world, with your family or others in your life (work, community, etc.). Everything that lies within the model represents you and how you are living and tending to yourself and your needs. Fill in the sections and make notes accordingly. Also take note if there is an area or areas that are in need of more support, or continued growth.

SPIRITUALITY

Spirituality is a topic that is deeply personal to each individual. There are many different beliefs, thoughts, traditions, and ways to honor what feels right to you and your family. I believe there is beauty and significance in each religion. Your version of tapping into your spirituality might be to go into the mountains to connect to your own divinity. For others, it might look much more traditional and take place in a church or place of worship. For others yet, it might be keeping your own council and sitting in silence in your home, garden, or among the trees. Finding a place where you can breathe, find that inner peace, and feeling of connection is powerful.

However you choose to connect to a higher power, and whatever name resonates highest for you, whether it be Creator, Spirit, God, Goddess, or Mother Nature is part of your personal path. Honor your own journey and don't think less of others who are not walking the same path as you in this way, perhaps they are meant to walk a very different walk. Also, don't be afraid to do some spiritual exploration. If you've always practiced in the same way, try something new or open your mind to learn a different way of connecting. Lean in; don't live in fear here. Fear and judgement strip you of your power and your brilliance. Celebrate the many ways there are to connect with others and a higher power at the same time.

If you don't consider yourself spiritual, honor your present state and where you are without judgment. You are right on time in life, things will unfold as they are meant to. Trust in that. Extend love to your neighbor and honor the differences. Don't let a divide happen. There has certainly been much division and conflict over religion for millennia. Perhaps it is time to lay down the anger and judgement and step into a place of more love, compassion, and understanding for others. This will serve all of humanity in a much deeper way, will enrich our families, and teach our children better ways of seeing their neighbors who might be vastly different from them.

I have always felt there is a higher power–something greater than all–but most of my life, I have had a hard time expressing my spirituality and finding a setting that felt right to me. However, in the last seven years I started to honor that I need spirituality in my life as a grounding chord, especially while raising my children. It is a place for me to find peace and respite, and it renews my drive and my motivations as a parent and as a person. My main place to renew is with my morning meditations, but I occasionally will seek out a church in the middle of the day when it is empty and sit there to find solace and connect to Source. Additionally, I do appreciate joining in church service from time to time and connecting with community in that way. There is a richness in sharing communally and I do find peace and renewal here.

I also have found deep personal healing when I have been

blessed to participate in Native American sweat lodges. Sweat lodges are so sacred, and I always enter and exit a slightly different person, as they are so meaningful and have enriched my spirituality in beautiful ways that have helped me continue to **grow**. Retreats and finding a spiritual community can also be very meaningful and nourishing, and I have found a beautiful sense of ease and belonging here, as well.

I believe we are all connected, and that the struggles we face around the world stem from this illusion of separateness that keeps us from recognizing how incredible and how important each spirit is on Earth. I'm at a point in life where I've come to feel we are all a little right and a little wrong in whatever beliefs we hold to be true, as no one has all the answers here. It is the Great Mystery of life.

We can accomplish much more together than we ever could alone, and we are all more alike than we remember. We need to honor one another and celebrate the richness of difference to find ways to work in harmony. In fact, I am of the mind there has never been a time when the world has experienced such hunger for more compassion, acceptance, love, and understanding of our neighbors. Treat strangers like you would your child; with love, respect, and tender care, even if you don't think they deserve it. You never know the struggles of another. We truly are all in this together, so why not honor that? One of my greatest wishes is that we might begin to see one other with endless love, and that peace and understanding will prevail and touch every corner of the globe, kissing every face. These teachings begin at home.

REFLECT

1. Do you have a regular meditation or spiritual practice? If not, is this something you are open to exploring? Why or why not?

2. How do you find stillness in life? How does it support your role as a parent?

3. How do you connect to your spirituality? If spirituality is not your thing, how do you make time for finding ease and peace in your life?

Chapter 9: Wellness

"Take care of your mind, your body will thank you. Take care of your body, your mind will thank you," - Debbie Hampton

With the workload of being a parent, it is crucial you support your physical body with fuel that will nourish and help you maintain your stamina and health, as well as give you endurance. Strive for a state of wellness in your life by being aware of what you put in and onto your body in the form of food, drink, substance, and product. If you feed and fuel your body with clean, whole foods and products, you will feel better and will also be more properly nourished and tended to. I personally limit alcohol, avoid eating processed food or using products loaded with chemicals and dyes (read the labels), and instead opt for organic or local products and foods whenever possible. I also aim to use cleaning products in our home that are natural and eco-friendly and strive to move my body every day because these all make such a difference for my mind, body, and spirit. Making these choices helps me show up as the best version of myself and support me at the highest level.

USE CLEAN PRODUCTS

While it is important to be mindful of what we put in our bodies in the form of food and drink, it is equally important what we put on it. Our skin is the largest organ of our body. We should be cognizant of what we apply to it, as it has the potential to impact your whole system. Often there is a tendency for people to not read the fine print or even have an awareness of chemicals that are present in the majority of products available on the market. It is worth taking a peek at products in your home such as home cleaning products, shampoo and conditioner, fragrance, sunscreen, makeup, and lotion. A great resource for educating yourself further is visiting ewg.org.

One of my biggest cringes (truly a deep concern) is when I see little kids getting slathered in sunscreen that is laden with chemicals. While it is important to have a sun barrier when out in the sun, I advocate for using all-natural sunscreen, using sun shirts and hats, and perhaps not going out in the heat of the day to avoid the most intense rays. I recognize the importance of protecting skin and keeping your body as safe as possible, but in the attempt to prevent skin cancer from the sun, many instead opt to apply known and possible carcinogens directly onto the body to no fault of their own.

Some of the most harmful chemicals found in sunscreens appear to be avobenzone, oxybenzone, octinoxate, and homosalate, based on current research. Benzene is another chemical worth mentioning because it is a volatile chemical compound found in some sunscreens that can influence cancer risk and impact immediate health. Benzene is not a standard ingredient in sunscreen, but I mention benzene because there are sunscreens that have been contaminated by benzene, even though it was not intentionally added. There is a theory being tested that certain compounds might mix to form benzene, especially in some of the spray-propellant sunscreens, but research is pending.

According to the CDC, "Benzene is known to cause cancer in humans. Yale Medicine (MacMillan, 2022) further explains, [benzene] is a highly flammable chemical that is a natural part of crude oil, gasoline, and cigarette smoke and is used to make plastics, nylon, and synthetic products." *Yikes*! We know there are chemicals in some sunscreens that are carcinogens, yet there is recommendation, encouragement, and allowance for these products to be used by adults and children alike.

There finally seems to be some traction taking place where more knowledge is finally coming to the surface, but this is still slow going. Additionally, there have been some recalls recently because more knowledge is coming to the surface about the harm these products can cause consumers. More education and awareness of this is vital so people can make smarter, more healthful decisions for their own bodies, their children's bodies, and the environment.

Finally, sunscreens laden with harmful chemicals not only impact humans, but they also have been found to impact coral reef systems in the ocean. According to the National Ocean Service (N.O., 2018), oxybenzone (which is found in over 3,500 sunscreen products worldwide), has been found to cause coral bleaching, disrupt coral reproduction, and damage coral DNA. If this chemical has the power to do this level of damage to the reef systems, imagine what it could be doing to the human body.

In the spirit of remembering that we all are connected, this extends beyond the human family to the natural world in which we inhabit. Choices we make for ourselves and our children do impact the world around us for better or for worse, so make time to do some personal research about what products (not just sunscreen, but skincare, hair, cleaning, and body products) are clean and safe for use. Your health and longevity for yourself and your family depend on it. Bringing a level of consciousness to personal choices will be impactful and helpful to you on your journey.

ALCOHOL

I debated whether or not to mention alcohol as it is a bit of a hairy subject, but since it has impacted our country and many individuals on such a wide and deeply personal scale, I couldn't refrain from at least mentioning it briefly (the nurse in me also wants to educate). It is also paramount to have more understanding and awareness here as a parent, because the more you know, the more you can release habits or tendencies that are not helpful or supportive to you or your family members. In doing so, it will allow for more wellness to show up in your life and help you continue to **grow**. People love to drink in our country, and honestly in many other countries as well. It is seen as pleasurable socially, it is incorporated into many holidays and pastimes and is a totally accepted social norm. I sincerely believe that when you are raising your kids, if you can work to reduce or eliminate alcohol from your life, you will be able to meet the best version of your parenting self every day.

Parents walk such a tightrope trying to keep it all together, and maintaining this purity on top of that can be particularly challenging, especially at the end of a long day or work week with many different issues pulling at you from every direction. However, instead of reaching for a stiff drink to unwind, try running a hot bath and light a candle. If baths aren't your thing, then play music, make art, watch a movie, do yoga, or go for a walk. There are many ways to unwind that don't require you altering your mental state to find that feeling of decompression. Put down the crutch that might be your nightly go-to and try something different. It can change your life and can help you become an even brighter version of your already incredible self. This doesn't mean you have to give up enjoying a drink or going out and being social, but rather if it has become your nightly routine to reach for your favorite bottle of wine or the like, see if you can shift gears and lean on this less frequently.

What we put into our body translates into what comes out, and not just physiologically. Even one glass of wine or beer alters your brain chemistry and impacts the way you feel the next day. It also impacts your mood, reactions to others, irritability level, and your quality of sleep. What I have found in raising our children is that I feel like the best version of me when I do not drink at all. In fact, I've come to love not drinking. I used to enjoy going out and being just as social as the next person, but with motherhood came a new set of rules and requirements–the biggest one being "on" for my children whenever they need me. That requires me to be operating at a high level. I am not into extremes in any direction per se, and so I like to leave a little wiggle room for an occasional glass of wine or beverage on special outings, as it can be nice to savor or celebrate festive occasions, and this works for me. You know your limits best, so check in with what this might look like for you and your family.

Being a parent is like being an Olympic athlete, except you have a way more intensive training schedule and it's called being on 24/7. Some might not appreciate this comparison, but I truly don't know a sport or profession that you are required to be on duty or in training around the clock, 365 days a year for 18 years! That is in many ways unreasonably a lot! On top of this comes the financial burden, along with no medals, no awards, no salary… you get the drift. I bow down to each of you out there trying your best to raise up this next generation. Well done, and major high fives all around. With this high level of expectation, commitment, and responsibility on your part, it will help you immensely if you can learn to live in a cleaner state.

Work towards living and parenting from a place of personal wellness. Get to know yourself fully and be with yourself, even if it feels like a hot mess some days. The more comfortable you are with yourself exactly as you are, the better able you will be at becoming more in sync with your natural rhythms. You might also find how incredible it can be to live and operate from a space of more clarity. Sometimes it's hard to really get to know yourself and easier to disconnect, but I encourage you to get to know the most beautiful version of you that often hides behind your facade. You might just like what you find. It is also an incredible way to reconnect with your inner child because you are living in alignment with more innocence and purity.

If this notion seems way out in left field, I encourage you to try going without a substance you rely on for two weeks and see if you notice a difference in the way you feel, the way you wake up feeling more refreshed, the way you parent, and the way you interact with others. I inadvertently gave up coffee this way, which was a major love of mine for many years. After two weeks, I switched to drinking green tea and haven't looked back. Don't get me wrong, when my husband makes his coffee in the morning, the smell still goes straight to my brain stem and there is a deep love of the essence that is coffee, but I do not miss drinking it. I actually always felt a bit muddy drinking coffee (that's the best way I know how to describe it), but with green tea, there is more clarity, and it feels cleaner in my body. Do some personal exploration here and really see if you are willing to give something up that isn't serving you in a totally divine way. Keep in mind that what feels clean to you may be different than what others experience.

I also want to provide some statistics about alcohol because these numbers speak for themselves to highlight what is going on, and it is not pretty. It is also helpful to keep in mind that these are only the United States statistics and do not take into account the global situation.

According to the National Institute on Alcohol Abuse and Alcoholism:

- 10.5% (7.5 million) children under the age of 17 are living with a parent who has alcohol use disorder (AUD is characterized by the inability to stop or control alcohol use, even when it is having an impact socially, in the workplace or having health consequences).
- Alcohol-related driving incidents in 2019 accounted for 28% of total driving-related deaths.
- The economic burden on the United States in 2010 was $249 billion dollars related to alcohol misuse (75% of this total is from binge drinking).
- Alcohol accounts for about 18.5% of emergency room visits annually and 22.5% of overdose deaths related to prescription opioids.
- In 2019, it was reported that 414,000 adolescents between the ages of 12-17 suffered from AUD.
- In 2019, 14.5 million people ages 12 and up had AUD.
- "An estimated 95,000 people (approximately 68,000 men and 27,000 women) die from alcohol-related causes annually, making alcohol the third-leading preventable cause of

death in the United States. The first is tobacco, and the second is poor diet and physical inactivity."

These are sobering statistics. We have a problem, but we don't really like to talk about it. I even found myself wanting to shy away from this subject, but realized knowledge is power and the more you know, the more you can be co-creators in shaping your reality. I'm not here to tell you how to live or what to believe, I am simply sharing powerful facts so that you can have a clearer picture of how alcohol is impacting our society, our culture, and our children. You get to draw your own conclusions about whether alcohol is helping or hurting our people.

When I see these statistics, it helps to put a major spotlight on the fact that people are suffering and likely hurting on a deep emotional level. These numbers are beyond moving, and it inspires me to want to work harder as a woman and mother to help illuminate a path that is less painful and traumatic for others. Empowering yourself and being mindful of how you intentionally choose to live is key to breaking free of these current trends. I believe people should make the choices in life that feel best for them, and I am so thankful to live in a country where we all have the freedom of choice. This is a major blessing often overlooked.

Many can and do find balance socially and have no trouble

here, but for others, substance abuse is a real struggle that causes real pain to themselves and their family. It is not about living a totally purist lifestyle, it is about making choices as a parent not only for yourself, but for those you love the most. What I am trying to do is stoke your inner fire and inner knowing so you can help shape a reality you are proud of for you, your family, and your community. If this is striking a note for you or is something that you struggle with and would like to improve, start thinking about taking steps to free yourself of what does not serve you (this may require you to seek professional help).

Finally, the things your children witness impact their future behavior and what they see as normal. They are always watching, so do your best to set the stage for a healthy and well-adjusted home life, and practice self-awareness here. Your personal choices, habits, and attitude all make such a difference. The choices you make and model are working to shape how your child behaves in school, how they present to the world, how they learn to navigate relationships, and how they respond when faced with making difficult decisions in life. Remember your blessings daily, remember the lessons you most want to impart on your family, and be the role model your children can depend on and learn from.

DRINK WATER

Water intake is such an important part of proper physical maintenance. While there are many drink choices in today's world, making sure you prioritize water intake throughout your day will keep your system supported and actually keep you healthier as well. This might seem pretty basic, but staying properly hydrated will give you a boost as a parent. According to Harvard medical school, most people should aim to drink at least four to six cups of water per day. Staying properly hydrated allows for "carrying nutrients and oxygen to your cells, flushing bacteria from your bladder, aiding digestion, preventing constipation, normalizing blood pressure, cushioning joints, protecting organs and tissues, regulating body temperature, and maintaining electrolyte balance," (Harvard Health, 2022).

I've grown up with "drink eight glasses of water per day" as the gold standard, but I think the ultimate goal here is to nourish and hydrate your body according to your needs. Each person will obviously have a slightly different water intake need and this should be individualized. It is not a one size fits all. Especially for parents who may have underlying health conditions or for people taking certain medications, drinking too much water can lead to water retention, which you need to be mindful of. Additionally, if you work out a lot, are super active, or if the weather is hot, you may need to increase your water intake to support you at a more optimal level.

The other thing to keep in mind here is that you are likely getting water from foods you eat and other beverages you are drinking throughout the day in addition to any water intake, which all work to help keep you hydrated. Compared to other beverages, water is by far the best way to support your system, stay healthy, and improve your energy as a parent.

TREAT YOURSELF

I am a dark chocolate kind of gal. I eat it almost every day. This is one of my favorite treats and a way that I infuse a little joy and self-care into my day. I am a firm believer that you should not skip treats. I am very health-minded, but I believe a little treat goes a long way and provides your spirit a boost and a moment of bliss, which are both things that parents can use more of. Instead of depriving yourself, just have something small that feels good. You can find the balance here.

Obviously too much of anything isn't ideal, so if you already tend to eat a lot of sugar or have a diet that is in need of some refinement, then work with care. You know your body best. Sugar can also become addicting, so be mindful. This is really about learning to carve out a moment to find a joy spot in your day. Think about ways you can pause or treat yourself to something that makes you smile and feel good because you are worth it, and you deserve the small pleasures in life that support you on your parenting path.

SEASONAL EATING

To ride the coat tails of Ayurveda, mentioned in the previous chapter, I also want to introduce the idea of seasonal eating. In Ayurveda, seasonal eating is encouraged because it supports your body in a way that is more aligned with the seasons. As a parent, eating food seasonally will support you in the most optimal way, will help you feel better, and will give you a leg up while you are chasing your munchkin. It also is a great preventative health measure to take and can make you feel better while you are eating your food. For example, you wouldn't want to be eating chilled gazpacho soup in the dead of winter or eating hot, thick stew in the middle of August when the weather is sweltering.

There is a reason you naturally are drawn to cooling foods in the summer and heartier, warmer, and more dense foods in the winter. Where you live on the planet, traditions, holidays, and time of year all impact what you crave and what your body might desire or need for support. There also is an emotional and biological connection associated with eating food that is worth making note of as well. If you have had positive memories of foods at certain times of the year, you are more likely to opt for those foods again. Additionally, eating locally and seasonally leaves a smaller carbon footprint and the food usually tastes better because it is in season.

I believe so deeply that eating in sync with whatever season you find yourself in will benefit your physical and mental body. There are plenty of guides and ideas about seasonal foods to match with your dosha if you want to explore it further.

EXERCISE

Finding an exercise that compliments your current workload at home is something worth exploring. If you have an enormous job on the home front, you need movement daily that is compatible to help you move the energy out of your system in a healthy and intentional way. For example, I have found that I need some higher intensity workouts to move my energy because I have the intensity of raising four boys at home. There is plenty of literature out there about the need for regular exercise, which is great, but what I want to drive home is the need to have a true match of lifestyle to physical movement. If you aren't striking the balance of parenting stress and demands with an appropriate physical outlet, then energy can build in your system and sometimes it comes out in an unhelpful way. Try to move your energy in a way you intentionally want to, so it doesn't end up moving you in a way you might not want or feel proud of at the end of the day.

My go-to's are hot yoga, yoga sculpt, Pilates, running, hiking, biking, or hitting the gym and lifting weights. I personally appreciate variety, and I like to mix and match to vary what I am doing. Splashing in variety and change provides more balance to my mind, body, and spirit. If your home tends to be quieter and the energy requirement less, you might benefit from tai chi or gentle yoga, walking, or the like. You know your body best, you should take time to assess what feels like a compliment to your parenting home life and your current level of health. If you are unsure or have further questions, consulting a healthcare professional is always an excellent option.

Another consideration related to exercise and movement is to have a routine with your workouts, or something to look forward to weekly. I aim to move daily, but I do take days off for sure, as it is healthy and important to give your body time to rest. The CDC recommends, "150 minutes of moderate intensity physical activity and two days of muscle strengthening activity" weekly for adults. This translates into two and a half hours of physical activity per week, plus two days of muscle strengthening. An example of a balanced way to break this up could be:

- Monday: one hour trail running or hiking
- Tuesday: half hour weight training, at home or gym

- Wednesday: one hour yoga or Pilates
- Thursday: half hour weight training, at home or gym
- Friday: one hour spin class
- Saturday: family time-playing at the park, taking a family hike, or engaging in a fun activity of your choice
- Sunday: rest and rejuvenate

If you don't have the luxury of alone time or the ability to make it to a gym, no problem! Get creative; you can skip to school with your kids, do stairs at work, take a 20 minute walk after a meal, go for a run in your neighborhood, do yoga in your living room, etc. It really doesn't matter how you move, just that you make the time to move. You can also include your children in some of your exercise regimen if time and schedules allow. I do think it's healthy for you to have some of this allotted time as "me-time," meaning you are on your own for this, but infusing some family time is also healthy, as it can allow for some great bonding time and provides excellent role modeling for your kids. Promoting a healthy lifestyle and practicing self-care in this way will keep you moving in the right direction and keep your energy flow focused where you want it; in a place that is building you up and giving you vitality to parent with more intention and love.

MOVE THAT ENERGY

In addition to the exercise component, I want to offer some creative ways to move your and your child's energy when things become stagnant or tricky. Moving your energy every day in a healthy way is crucial because if you don't, there is a tendency for it to build up and come out in a negative way. Say you've hit a wall with your child, have had a tough week, or have been in a disagreement of some kind. Please consider using the following ideas for making a breakthrough or simply finding more joy and maybe even some giggles with your child:

- **Drum**- Grab some bongos, djembe or a frame drum and find some rhythm with your child to loosen up any tension that has been building.
- **Dance with your kids**- Turn up the music and really get your boogie on. This can be especially freeing, both for your body and mind and it's really a fun avenue for outward expression in a free form way.
- **Scavenger Hunt**- Set up scavenger hunts in your home to help bring some playfulness into your routine. It could be as simple as leaving clues for your child to find their lunchbox in the morning, or setting up a list of items to look for when you go out for a nature walk. These are both ways to make mundane activities a little

more fun for both you and your child.

- **Yell therapy**- Yell into a pillow if you can't be loud in your neighborhood or home, and include your kids in this. I know how suffocating it can feel to always try to communicate quietly, especially if there is emotion involved. It is healthy to get it out and I encourage the movement of your voice in this way. Simply yelling "AHHHHH" can do wonders for your mental health and can free you from any pent-up emotion you may be storing in your physical body. Doing this out in nature is also another great option.
- **Take a break from your child**- Try to do this daily if you can. This isn't an option for all parents, and I have so much respect for parents who don't have the support they need to take a break, but it is healthy for you and for them to have a little space on a regular basis. Even if it's for 15 minutes and you walk two blocks, make the time.
- **Create Space**- Make time to be one-on-one with your kids if you have more than one child. We did this when our boys were young, and it was incredibly valuable time spent, both for our sons and us as parents. We called it "special time." Sometimes your children all get lumped together; this is unfortunate because one-on-one bond-

ing can cause dynamic shifts that are huge when you make time to get to know your child as an individual. I can't stress enough how rewarding this is. It is truly a must do.

CHANGE

Additionally, I want to mention something I recently noticed in my local gym. There was a sign on the wall that read, "if it doesn't challenge you, it won't change you" (Fred DeVito). Coming from a place of trying to apply that to the parenting realm, I sat with this statement for a whole afternoon because it shook something loose in me. I was left wondering, *is that really true*? When I look back at some of my most intense periods of personal growth, challenge was definitely a factor, and while the metamorphosis isn't always easy, those moments of challenge can help you grow in ways you couldn't imagine beforehand. Whether it be tied to your physical workout and pushing yourself to reach new heights and **grow** or the actual challenge of what it takes to raise your children, change will surely follow suit if you make the time and put the energy forth to let the process change you for the better.

This is also an excellent time to re-evaluate whether or not you are carving out "me time" and if you aren't, consider starting. You can start small and build from there, it will change your life and enhance who you are as an individual separate from who you are when you are with your child or family. It's critically important to know who you are. Challenge yourself to rise to the occasion to honor your personal temple and make this a priority. When you align with health and intentional living, your life will flourish in gorgeous ways.

MIRROR-EFFECT

Your kids are uniquely themselves and ultimately walking their own path. While you are responsible for helping to shape and set parameters, your children are responsible for their own life choices, and this is not on you. However, what I have noticed is the way I show up for my kids is what I get mirrored back. Alignment, for example, is about bringing your best self to the table intentionally, as often as you can remember. When I am living in alignment, meaning I am showing up and parenting from the best place and being the person I know I am capable of being, alignment is what I get back from my boys. When I am out of alignment, I also get that mirrored back.

Your children pick up on your energy, meaning what you have to give and what you bring to the table. This for me has been such a rich learning experience, and when I am having an off week, I can see how my presence and choices can have rippling effects for better or worse. When I remember the power and pull I have, and that I always have a choice of how I want to live and role-model, I can shift out of whatever it is that holds me back and find my center. I try to live from my center every day, because when I am centered, I am in balance and in harmony and can share that balance with my family.

My children teach me, and I teach my children, and we help one another grow. I try to celebrate our imperfections and learn from them because what else can you do? It becomes counterproductive to perseverate and beat yourself up about the realities of your life, many of which are out of your control. We need to love every inch of who we are, including the shadows and bright spots because they work together to make you, you. The best gift you can give yourself is a big dose of self-compassion mixed with love, and sprinkle in a sense of humor about the madness and insanity that is life and oftentimes parenting.

Learn to treat yourself like you treat others. Make your inner voice lovingly say positive truths that add value to your existence. Anything less is taking away from your time here as a parent. Be sure to clean your mirror daily, so that what it reflects back to you is something you are proud of.

REFLECT

1. Are you aware of any trends or gaps where you may need more or less to support your system? Take time to reflect

on your dietary intake daily. Keep a written log for a week and track what and when you are eating and drinking.

2. What exercise and/or holistic regimen do you currently have? Is it complimenting your parenting home-life and helping you to move energy in a healthy way? If not, how can you implement changes?

3. What are your thoughts and feelings about using clean products in your life? Is this something you are open to exploring? Why or why not?

Chapter 10: Inner Child

"While we try to teach our children all about life, our children teach us what life is all about." - Angela Schwindt

Children are some of the biggest gurus on this planet. Oxford Languages defines guru as "a spiritual teacher, especially one who imparts initiation." I am using the term guru loosely here, as it has become more socially acceptable to do so. Traditionally, this term was used for a teacher who has deep knowledge and the ability to lead others to enlightenment. I don't know about you, but becoming a parent has been the most intense initiation I have ever experienced to date. My children have taught me more about myself, my strengths, my weaknesses, my capacity to love, and my desire to grow, change and persevere than any other humans to date. They have in many ways enlightened my path and have helped me grow in ways I likely would not have, had I not stepped into motherhood. You might consider thanking your son or daughter for all the rich teachings they have brought to your life. Share with them your gratitude. It's time to honor children for all the enlightenment and teachings they bring to our lives.

Society often looks down on or is of the mindset that children need to listen to their elders or need to be the ones in training (which is in many ways accurate). Perhaps though, we have gotten it slightly wrong and need to do more listening; maybe lay off the top-down approach a bit. Don't get me wrong, children need guidance and structure to learn to respect their elders, which is your job as a parent, but there are many instances where we interject when perhaps we do not need to. There are many hours in a day and many opportunities to practice learning from your child. This may sound like a non-conventional theory, but if you give them an opportunity to teach you what they know or how they see the world, it might give you a better perspective as a parent. It might also spark your inner child again and light you up in ways you might not remember.

Kids are incredibly intuitive and excel at living in the moment. They tell it how they see or feel things, and often do not work with a filter for better or worse, depending on the timing. Children have a curious nature and are constantly exploring, taking in the world around them with eyes and hearts of wonder. They are creative and open-minded because they haven't built up walls or layers that come with the passing of time and lived experience. It begs you to ask them to "tell me more," so that you can learn from what comes so naturally to them.

Many of these positive qualities become dingy as we age. We don't play; we stop being curious, using our imagination, and living in the moment. Instead, many are hyper focused on being the provider, working, and stressing about all the million and one details of what it takes to raise a family. In the process, their own child-like sense of wonder and awe is forgotten.

Many of the qualities we are seeking to offset the unhappiness we might feel as adults and as parents (mindfulness and being in the now) we can learn from our children. Watch your child at work. Watch them without the lens of the parent for an afternoon and see them in their element. Watch them with their friends on the playground when there are no parents guiding play or intervening. Witness them being in the moment, using their imagination, and making friends without judgement, and see the innate beauty that is your child.

Recovering and reconnecting with your own inner child will benefit you immensely as a parent because it will help you parent with more joy. It will also help you find more ease with your child because you will be showing up with more understanding and awareness. If you can re-kindle this internal remembrance, it can give you some sparkle back to your everyday. Wake up every morning and give thanks. Try to greet the day as if it was the first time you were gifted with the experience of being a parent. Don't cling to the past or continue re-hashing things that have already occurred with your children. Let these experiences go and continue to try and try again. When you cling to the past, you rob yourself and your children of the opportunity to start fresh every day. When you allow yourself and your loved ones to start anew, you can then show up in the present. When you are in the present moment, what a gift you are giving yourself, as well as your child and the world.

Anything or anyone who can take you off your center is a teaching. Honor that. I believe my children have been some of my greatest teachers and my gurus in this life. I have been totally humbled by my kids over and over and over. Just when I think I'm getting it down, they move the mark again, and I have to find a new way to do things and a new way to relate and meet their needs and my own as we continue grow and change together. It is this continual cycle of death and rebirth that happens so slowly that you don't even realize it's happening. Taking a moment to look back and reflect on where you've been will allow you to see this transformation in ways that you haven't, even when it's right in front of you.

My boys keep me on my toes and help me with my own inner growth, and remembering my inner child in ways that I will forever be grateful for. Benefits of being child-like are many and include being content, an intense desire to explore and seek adventure, the acceptance of others, believing in magic, having incredible resilience, being imaginative, innocent, energetic, and living simply. Quite frankly, it is just a whole lot more fun to channel your inner child than to move through the world as a burnt-out adult and parent. I also believe that the practice of honoring and remembering your inner child will not only help you parent better but likely will help you age better as well. It will keep you lighter and less wrapped up in your stories and stresses, which ultimately will benefit your mind, body, and spirit.

BRING THE MAGIC

I wholeheartedly believe in magic. I think it is all around us and available to anyone who wants more in their life. Learning to be open to magic and miracles is optional. Beyond just opening to magic, I encourage you to spread magic, far and wide. Be a magic maker and make your child's journey full of wonder, joy, and awe. When you live solely from a position of logic, reason, focus, and staying between the lines, you limit what is possible and what might be able to land for you if you let it. Sometimes there are things in life that aren't logical or even rational but happen anyway. Remember to have eyes to see, ears to hear, and a heart to feel the subtleties that are all around you. Don't stop believing.

A moment of magic for me happened shortly after my stepmother passed away. I was driving alone in my truck and "On the Wings of a Snow White Dove," a song that was played at her funeral, came on. Before her funeral, I had never heard this song in my life. To have it come through on the radio waves just a couple weeks after her passing felt like receiving magic and light from above. Sometimes you get those nods from the other side, and you can't explain them, but they are real and they are so meaningful. Don't discount what you can't explain. Make sure as a parent you don't forget to weave some magic and miracle-making into your life; be open to receive whatever form it shows up in.

ICE CREAM FOR BREAKFAST

I remember being at a Fourth of July parade with my family a few years back and there was an elderly man sitting on the sidewalk at about 8:30 a.m., eating an ice cream cone. He was happy. He was smiling, sitting in the sunshine, and he struck up a conversation with us. He actually began the conversation by singing us a song that was meaningful to him and then continued on to tell us he begins every morning with an ice cream cone. He reminded us that life is short, and he wanted to do things that brought him joy. My children were obviously impressed and a tad jealous that this man got to have ice cream every day for breakfast.

This interaction made me pause and do some reflection on the rules and regulations we impose on our reality and our children's realities that perhaps we don't always need to. My children are sad to report that they still don't get to start the day with ice cream cones, but they do have a mom that allows for wiggle room around things that can bend more than we think. This is a reminder to lighten up; don't always do everything by the books. Forge your own path and weave more delight in your life and in the lives of your children. *Why not*? I always appreciate when I receive teachings in the least likely places. Keep your heart and mind open to receiving lessons not only from your children, but from the world around you. You might just be amazed.

REFLECT

1. Who is your guru? Do you believe your child or children are your guru(s)? Why or why not?

2. What in your life has the ability to pull you off your center mark? How does this impact your ability to **grow**?

3. In what areas of your life can you nurture your inner child?

CHAPTER 11: CONSCIOUS PARENTING

"Conscious parenting is a game changer because it doesn't try to change the child, just ourselves as parents." - Shefali Tsabary

Conscious parenting is really about remembering your intention and awareness within yourself and around you when you show up for your family. I've already outlined what conscious parenting is previously, but I believe refreshing this concept is helpful in cementing it to your memory bank. Additional ways to support you and your consciousness in showing up the way you intend to includes getting organized, practicing positive reinforcement, collaborative problem solving, boundary setting, and remembering your motivations daily. Take a minute every day to remember your center and your reasons for doing what it is you are doing. This will help you continue to **grow**.

Get organized. Organization is a key ingredient to my success as a parent. Without organization, things go south–so to speak. Organization helps me prioritize what needs to get done, when it needs to get done by, and so on. I am also religious about making lists of what I need to do that day or week; it is amazing when I write out what needs to get completed, how much easier I am able to get it all accomplished. I literally cross items off one by one as I get them done and it energizes me to know I am accomplishing what I set out to do for the day. I am old school and use paper and pen, but I know many of you all probably prefer using your phone or device for this, and that is great. Whatever it takes for you to prioritize and organize your life and to-do lists, use it and use it often, as this will help you to **grow** immensely and will help you keep things moving in the right direction.

I am also a believer in cleanliness. Making your bed every morning and keeping your home clean will benefit you in ways that you might not even realize. Think of it as energy flow. If there are piles of clothes, boxes, and toys scattered everywhere, or a sink full of dishes, this is clogging your energy field. You know it's there in the back of your mind and that you should be getting to it, but when you don't, it silently gnaws at you, making you less effective at other things you are working on. Every time you walk by the mess you think, *I should clean this up*, but when you don't, you are losing some of your ability to be productive in other areas of your life.

Living in or around a mess can actually impact your mental and physical health. On a positive note, if you can bring yourself to honor your home and get those piles, messes, and overflowing closets cleaned up, it's like doing an internal cleanse as well. You literally will feel more empowered and free, and will love being in your space much more. Your kids will also benefit from having a clean home; it will teach them the skills they need as they grow and ultimately set out on their own. Additionally, recruit your children to help out with household chores to help ease your workload. Having weekly chores for them to tend to can help your child **grow** and learn responsibility, both personally and as part of a family unit. The process of your child helping out will also teach them the importance of learning to manage their space and take pride in their home environment. Take some time to clean the house but remember to find the balance here and not take it to extremes.

Finally, work to release any resistance you may have towards tending to your daily routine. Doing your chores with a good attitude and even a smile will change your life. If you are showing up for your kids crabby, agitated, or overwhelmed with what you have to accomplish every day, you are creating your own misery. Misery breeds more misery. I'm not saying you have to parent like Mary Poppins but try to view your role as a parent as a gift, instead of a burden. Mind over matter here.

Many parents lose themselves and their good attitude in the process of child rearing. After a few years into starting a family, or maybe even sooner, you might be experiencing feelings of burnout. If you are doing the dishes for the seventh time in one day, tackling a mountain of laundry, or changing diapers over and over and over, try to remind yourself that you have been so blessed to be in the presence of such a tiny little miracle. Do your chores with love and a twinkle in your eye. You have what it takes, and when you bring joy into your job it makes everything feel better for you and your family.

Train your mind to stay where you put it. If you find yourself in the category of having a bad attitude more times than not as you work in the home, then haul yourself out of the irritation trenches, pull up your bootstraps and re-harness your good attitude. Learning to release any negativity here will change your perspective and radically shift your role as a parent. You've got this.

POSITIVE REINFORCEMENT

The primary aim of positive reinforcement is to focus on increasing a desired behavior. Oftentimes, using positive reinforcement is more effective than punishment or negative reinforcement because it makes the child feel better, more supported, and more connected with the parent or adult providing the reinforcement. When you lean on positive reinforcement as a means of guiding your child, you are encouraging good behavior which is ultimately less damaging to your child's confidence, self-esteem, and growth.

For me, offering positive reinforcement is what I strive for as a parent. It is my starting point. Candidly, I have a hard time adhering to this method strictly. I am a work in progress in this area, and that is okay. I always aim to start from a place of offering positive reinforcement as my go-to. However, I've found that depending on different life circumstances, and with the task of juggling four rowdy boys, sometimes consequences or loss of privileges seem to be the most effective way to truly get my children's attention. It doesn't mean that you should lead with consequences as your primary means of delivery.

I am still promoting positive reinforcement as your guiding light, but sometimes despite your best efforts, negative reinforcement is where things may land. As with all parenting strategies, strive for balance here. I share my personal experience because one size does not fit all and while you intend to show up for you kids coming from a place of offering positive reinforcement, know that sometimes positivity might not always be the most effective route to re-direct undesired behavior. Use your intuition and inner knowing on the correct path to take, you know best on what feels most appropriate in any given situation.

Positive reinforcement is something to work towards. It doesn't mean you will always end up there, but certainly try to give it a go and perhaps consider it as your home base. This style of parenting will help your child know that they are loved, supported, and important. It will help them strive to meet their own goals, boost morale, help them with growth and development, and minimize negative behaviors. Positive reinforcement also strengthens your child's competence and autonomy, which will benefit them their whole life.

This method strengthens your bond with your child because it feels good to both parties; you, the one offering praise and encouragement and your child, who will appreciate your support and be more motivated to continue making the right choices with the affirmation they are receiving from you. It is a terrific way to model leadership, as well as setting the stage for behavior that is appreciated in the home.

PRACTICE POSITIVE REINFORCEMENT

You might be wondering how to implement positive reinforcement in your home, so here are some ways you can start practicing this style of parenting. You can try words of encouragement for a job well done, utilizing a star chart or a marble jar (which also can piggyback on goal setting if there is a task, chore, homework, or otherwise to work towards), giving a high five or "knucks," as we call fist bumps in our home, displaying art or projects they have completed at school, physical praise in the form of a hug, telling your child "well done," celebrating wins and participation in events (remember it's not just about winning or the outcome, but the experience) such as going out for ice cream or a pizza party after sporting events, doing all their music lessons on time for the month, etc.

While it is so important to rally around your child for a job well done, don't forget to offer support when there is failure. Sometimes your child will experience failure, whether it be failing a test, having a tough day in sports, hitting a rough patch with friends, or not hitting their personal mark or yours. In the face of failure, continue to be a rock for them and offer positive reinforcement and encouragement to keep at it. This will help them know you are there for them regardless of wins or failures.

The other piece that is essential in using positive reinforcement is consistency and frequency. Ideally, you should be dedicated to this style of parenting, otherwise it's not going to have the same impact. If you use positive reinforcement for a week and then stop for a while and try to pick it back up at a later date, the results won't be what you want them to be. It is more helpful and effective to make a commitment to this path for it to work optimally. This might require patience and determination on your part to stick it out, as you might not get results right out of the gate. Each child is so vastly different, and all have different needs, motivations, drives, and personalities to factor into this equation.

Like attracts like, so while your child might not always have behavior that you feel like celebrating or rewarding, work to ignore the behavior you don't want and really make clear the behavior you do want by rewarding the correct actions. The more positive you can be on a regular basis, the more it will transfer to your child and help them keep a more positive, grounded, and well-rounded attitude towards life, school, and home. This type of parenting also works to build self-esteem, helps empower your child to be the best version of themselves, and it actually helps you as the parent in the process. Make your positivity and kindness contagious, so that it illuminates your home and all those you come in contact with. This is a tremendous gift you can give to yourself and others.

In our home, we have implemented most of the examples I just provided over the years. These examples do work, and they help encourage positive behavior and uplift our boys. When I offer positive reinforcement as a mom, it feels good. I'm helping to encourage the behavior and actions that are wanted and at the same time giving our boys a personal confidence boost when they are hitting the mark, so they feel good. Positivity breeds positivity, so remember this as you work to help shape your little one. Remember to practice self-kindness with yourself if you miss your intended mark; we are only human. Feed your child light and encouragement and watch them **grow** and **glow**.

COLLABORATIVE PROBLEM-SOLVING METHOD

Teamwork makes the dream work. I love this expression and use it with my husband and friends often. While I usually am referring to sharing duties and relying on teamwork to get all of the daily activities done, in this instance I am referring to working to make your child part of the team. Collaborative problem-solving method is a diamond in the rough.

According to Think: Kids Massachusetts General Hospital, this theory is rooted in the idea that a child who is having undesirable behavior is really misunderstood and can then be mistreated as an outcome. This theory is based around the concept that a child does well when they can. It speaks to the notion that a child isn't simply misbehaving because they want to but rather that they lack the skills to behave. Misbehavior is not a willful action, but rather an undeveloped skill set.

Within this theory it is also thought that children are already trying hard, even if it doesn't appear that way. The first step is to identify any triggers to a child's misbehavior and then start to develop a plan for skill building.

Oftentimes there is imposition of adult will here and parents are forcing their will on the child, which can lead to rebellion and worsening behavior. If this is the case, identify it and then work on ways to improve, both for your child's sake and your own. As a parent, think of it in broader terms and try to put yourself in your child's shoes. Consider how it feels when other adults impose their will on you. It doesn't feel great and sometimes leads to resentment or feelings of wanting to rebel. Your child feels the same way, they just can't verbalize it the way you can and so they act out instead.

Once you've put in time to identify triggers and have done goal setting on needed skill development, work to problem-solve collaboratively with your child. Make them a team player and get them invested in the process of growth. Working as a team will help strengthen your relationship, will work to improve any behavior issues, and skills will naturally improve in the process. You also might consider lowering your expectations on behavior that is a lower priority while your child works to improve any skills that have been identified as needing improvement.

Lowering expectations for a time can take pressure off of you, the parent, and allow your child a little more spaciousness to start down a more solid path. What I especially appreciate about CPS is that it helps you learn to meet your child where they are versus expecting them to be where you think they should be. This is powerful. Keeping this in mind and approaching behavior development as a team will definitely help you and your child continue to **grow** and learn together.

POSITIVE PARENT ACRONYM

P- Peaceful Heart: When you show up for your child with a peaceful heart, you are meeting them with your best self. Holding peace in the heart space helps you to remember your center. When you find your center, you come from a place of balance and have a better perspective on situations as they arise and as life ebbs and flows. This one is closely aligned with remembering your consciousness.

A- Authentic: Authenticity is a big one! When you introduce your kids to your real self, what a gift you are giving them. Being real about who you are, what is important to you, and what motivates you as a parent and a person is invaluable for your child to witness. This is also the place where you remember to shed your ego as a parent and not worry so much about what others perceive from the outside, as this distracts from authentic parenting. Let your brilliance shine here to connect in a true and loving way.

R- Radiant: Parenting from a state of radiance is possible and attainable. The more you practice connected, conscious, and grounded parenting, the more radiant and joyful you become. When you drop reaction, let go of habits that don't serve, eat the right foods, and move your body in ways that support and uplift, you will become more radiant to your child and to others you come in contact with. You will feel better, and you will parent from a space of more awareness, with more understanding of yourself in the process.

E- Energized: Parenting can feel like an energy drain some days, as you give and give and give your energy away to others. While the giving of energy might not cease once you've learned how to be more conscious as a parent, the way you distribute your energy can shift to make life feel less exhausting. You can work to re-organize the way you live daily and carve out more time to nourish yourself in the process of giving. Some days will allow for more of this re-fuel time than others but stay at it. Also, don't be afraid to say "no" to outside commitments that don't directly impact you or your family. As parents sometimes you take too much on and that can take away from your ability to carry out all the tasks being asked of you. Energize your life and re-prioritize if necessary.

N- Nirvana: I chose the word nirvana to infuse some humor here and keep it lighthearted. While you may not reach a state of nirvana while child rearing, it can be something to work towards. A state of bliss and perfect happiness might not be part of the practice of raising your young, but there are moments for sure of bliss and perfection along the path. Try to look for them. One of my favorite times of day to touch base with nirvana is morning snuggles with our kids. This is happening less as our children grow older, but our youngest is still up for some big cuddles, and I am grateful for this. Before the day starts and the energy is quiet, to have this shared space, closeness, and bonding time is my definition of perfection. Just being in each other's proximity in a way that is sweet, reciprocal, connected, undemanding, and pure; it doesn't get much better than that.

T- Thankful: Giving thanks daily is such a powerful practice. Give thanks and be grateful for the breath that moves in and out of your body and sustains your very life. Practice gratitude for your family and your community, giving thanks for access to clean water and food, for the sun, moon, and stars that shine brightly down upon us all, for all beings on this planet, for the natural world… you get the idea. Let gratitude be a guiding light on your parenting journey, it will uplift you and help you see more clearly when things get cloudy.

Share and teach gratitude to your children to help them practice being grateful and teaching simple phrases such as "thank you" can work wonders for them in their lives.

REALITY CHECK

While bringing your positive attitude and positive ideas to the table is a very important step in conscious parenting, sometimes it isn't enough to re-route your child in the direction you want them to go. If you hit points in the road that are particularly challenging to work through, just stay the course. Parenting is not all rainbows, deep breathing, and glitter. There are some serious dark clouds that roll through that you have to navigate whether you want to or not. You have to rise to the occasion and be a warrior and find your center to help you maintain your **glow** despite whether things are going well or not.

Sometimes your kids will scream at you, call you names, tell you they hate you, hit you, lie to you, steal from you, fight with their siblings, or behave in unruly and rebellious ways. Hold space for them and honor that this is part of their journey. It is the learning they are meant to experience, and not a personal attack on you. They have not developed the skills to self-regulate their emotions and behavior the way we wish they could sometimes. Children also feel safest at home with their mom, dad, or family, so this is where the beast comes out most often, for this very reason.

Having an awareness that your child comes from you but they are indeed their own person will allow for more understanding, especially when you hit bumps in the road. As much as you might want to mold and shape them, they ultimately have their own guiding light for what and who they are. This is important to remember, especially when they hit the age of having to make some of their own choices, and some of their choices are less than ideal. Be there for them as they grow, make mistakes, say hurtful things, and do things you perhaps wish they hadn't done. Love them through any hardship, whether it be a hardship they are facing or one they have imposed upon you.

BOUNDARY SETTING

Setting boundaries in your home will help your child have a solid grasp on wanted behavior and expectations. Boundary setting also assists your child in developing coping skills, teaching self-discipline, safety, and setting limits for themselves. Setting boundaries is healthy in relationships, both for you as a parent and for your children. It also allows room for a greater sense of identity, bringing into focus your own well-being, helping you to discover more about who you are and at the same time teaching your children a richer understanding of who they are as they grow. There are different boundaries worth considering, such as:

physical, emotional, time, sexual, spiritual, and financial boundaries. Additionally, when you are setting boundaries, work to do this when you are in a calm headspace and can devote time to clarify what it is you need and want in your life, especially as you guide your child to develop their boundaries as well. Starting from a centered place will help you navigate these waters with more intention, purpose, and clarity.

When setting boundaries, you first need to make time to consider what your personal limits are. Communicating those boundaries with your family and possibly others in your life will help to establish a baseline from which to operate in a healthy way. Upholding your boundaries and being consistent will help strengthen your own convictions and make it clear to those around you that your boundaries should be respected and honored. Boundary setting is a gift you give to yourself. For example, consider how much time you need alone and how much time you want to spend together as a family, and then make time to tend to both. Explore these different areas and be mindful in how you choose to set your limits. If you don't have boundaries currently established in your life, consider how this is impacting you as a parent.

Boundary setting has the ability to really help cement goodness in life, bring you more of what you desire, and shave off areas that are taking away from your experience. It is also important to remember that while you establish boundaries, your child might not always operate within this framework. I have found that the majority of the time they will, but your child is learning and growing and with this comes the testing of boundaries. Your children will test you, and not just once. When they test the boundaries and step outside the lines, work to guide them back by setting limits to help them remember your framework more clearly in the future.

When your children are little, boundary setting such as counting "one, two, three" and having them stop what they are doing before you get to three will help them re-direct their actions. This can be quite effective and is something I used when my kids were little. However, what I found was oftentimes instead of earning a "time-out" for naughty behavior, they usually really needed a "time-in." They were acting up because they wanted my attention. I worked to be mindful of this and meet them where they were as much as I could. As your child grows older, they will likely push back more and counting to three will lose its edge, so you have to rise and grow with your children by coming up with clever and thoughtful ways to create effective boundaries. Loss of screen time or loss of time with friends is powerful currency for older children today and this can be something to help keep your child operating from a place that is in alignment with the boundaries your family chooses to set.

Additionally, when the time comes and you are asked to set a consequence for your child's behavior, be mindful that the punishment or loss of privilege isn't punishing you as well. I have had to learn this along the way. Often when you are in the moment (reacting vs. pausing and responding) to whatever situation you find yourself in, you might say something to your child, such as "you are grounded for a week!" and later realize that consequence isn't practical or ideal for what you may have going on in your life and therefore hard to adhere to. **Stop** and think through the consequence and what you want to say before you open your mouth. If you can't have follow through then boundary setting becomes much less effective and less meaningful in teaching your child your expectations. It also teaches that mom or dad's boundary setting doesn't mean as much as it should, which probably isn't what you are going for.

While we are on the topic of boundary setting, I also want to briefly mention natural consequences. Natural consequences can be strikingly effective at helping your child take more ownership of responsibilities in their own life as they grow and develop. Natural consequences stem from your child's behavior and are not driven by parental involvement. This can be forgetting their coat, not completing homework, or forgetting their lunch. This in and of itself can teach your child to remember their items and teach them responsibility in remembering what they need. It also teaches them when they do not hit the mark or keep themselves organized there are natural consequences to their day.

The results are felt by your child and imprinting happens through cause and effect. If they forget their coat they will be cold, or if they forget to pack their lunch they likely will go hungry at lunch that day. This hopefully will help them remember to be more organized in the future and not repeat this choice or behavior again. For every cause, there is an effect. This also can be driven by other peers or even by society. Both boundary setting and natural consequences work to help your child find their way in the world.

THE PARENTING 12

While writing this book, I asked twelve different parents (both mothers and fathers) what the most important lesson they wanted to teach their child was. If there was one thing their child(ren) could take away and carry with them throughout their lives, what would it be? Here are the responses, which I have chosen to keep anonymous:

1. "Nothing that you say or do today in and of itself, is going to alter your child's behavior and because of this you need to let go of the situational stuff more…trying to change your child's behavior in one fell swoop is not practical or rec-

ommended. It's a continual molding and support system you put in place to help them grow and help them be who they innately are."

2. "I want my children to know that they are whole on their own, and to have faith in their own intuition. Of course I want them to be open and learn, but I want them to trust themselves for guidance. I also want them to know how important it is to connect with and show kindness to other living things."

3. "Resilience."

4. "If there's one thing I want my kids to know, it is to be a life-long learner, and never stop learning. Learning will spark your adventure, engage your mind, and feed your soul. Learn how to love. Learn how to fail. Learn how to take risks. Learn how to be still. Learn about yourself. Learn about others. Then learn about our world. Learn what makes you happy and what makes others happy. Learn how to get better at one thing, or everything. Learn how to pay attention: to your surroundings, to your people, to yourself. Learn what successful means: in relationships and in a healthy life. Then learn how to be successful at all of those, or one at a time. But, as soon as you think you

have something figured out, it will change. You will change, your life will change, your love will change, or your world will change. Trust that being a life-long learner will guide you. There's no end to learning, and there is always room to grow."

5. "Honesty."

6. "Make every decision out of love."

7. "Stay humble, be kind, always be truthful, having boundaries is healthy, and 'put your oxygen mask on first.'"

8. "Remain open-minded and curious to the world and others."

9. "The most important lesson for my children is for them to be true to themselves and valuing their self-worth."

10. "Honesty."

11. "That they know they are so loved."

12. "Kindness. To the plants, to the people, to the planet, to themselves, to the people they love, to the strangers on the street, to their elders."

I wanted to capture the essence of what feels most important for parents to instill in their children and felt it was important to have outside perspective in making this work I've been doing more meaningful and more well-rounded. Even though this is a small sample size, it gives you a flavor of what fellow parents are trying to pass on to the next generation. I wanted to spark thought and curiosity here. This is a major area to continue to **grow** as you contemplate what your personal response or priorities are.

What I appreciated most about this experience of reaching out to fellow parents was the feedback from a couple of them that this question was the catalyst for deeper discussion with their significant other and even with their children as they processed and thought about what the most important life lesson they wanted to pass on was. This was exciting and meaningful feedback because this is what I want to help fuel: reflection and more discussion on what matters most while parenting. When you take time to reflect and pause, it sure does help you **grow** and get more intentional in how you show up and what you are willing to work towards.

REFLECT

1. What is the most important life lesson you want to pass to your child(ren)? How does it compare or contrast to what these fellow parents shared?

2. How can positive reinforcement be used in your family? Journal or contemplate how to positively praise your child.

3. What is your personal definition of nirvana in your life? Are there any moments of perfection that rise up to meet you daily?

PART 4

GLOW

CHAPTER 12: RADIANCE

"If you want to give light to others you have to glow yourself."
- Thomas S. Monson

Seed your heart with radiance. Let this internal **glow** affect your external reality. Being radiant is not something to work towards, rather it is a state already there waiting for you to see what is innate. We are born with a pure nature, yet we often forget as we grow and become distracted by what life is asking of us, especially during the extended season of parenthood. See if you can return to this place of remembrance and trust that you are exactly where you are meant to be.

There are many different routes for finding your radiance and helping you to become luminous as a parent, but here are some of my favorite ways to attain this state: see the beauty all around you, honor imagination, keep dreaming, find intention, cultivate self-care and dedication, keep reminders, date nights, get in the water, continue to learn, and approach life with humor. Think of these offerings as recommendations for learning to make contact with the luminosity and radiance within yourself.

BEAUTY

Your world will open with new possibilities if you begin to see the beauty that is within as well as all around you. If your perception of your world feels less than ideal or overwhelming as a parent, then look for small things to bring light. Perhaps it is a smile from a stranger or the way your child will say something that brightens your day. If you are moving too fast, the small things go unnoticed and when you remember to slow down, your field of perception will broaden and become more sensitive, allowing you to see things that often you neglect to see.

Many of us are experts at taking so much for granted in our everyday reality. This isn't a shaming statement, but a statement to help you remember the beauty that lies within and all around you when you pause and take time to notice all the blessings you've been given, even if it feels like there aren't many. We all have something to be grateful for, so remind yourself there is endless beauty abound. Open your heart and eyes to see what you perhaps have been missing.

A couple of years ago, my youngest son was out in the

yard when I went to collect him for lunch. He was sitting in a tree and when I approached, he looked at me and said, "mom, trees have so much gratitude." This statement swept me off my feet. His depth, deep understanding, and insightfulness at such a young age struck deeper than what many adults can bring to the table. Such a simple statement, said with so much power, sincerity, and truth. I remember his words being my teaching for the day and it really lifted my heart to hear what he was feeling and being offered by the trees.

It is in the small things that larger things can begin to blossom. Look for beauty and radiance and that is what you shall see. Be open to receiving beauty. If you feel unworthy or that being in a state of beauty is out of reach for you, work to shift this, as we are all worthy of receiving and giving beauty away to others. Be mindful of where you put your attention and intention, as this is where energy will follow. Let your radiant spirit shine through.

HONOR

Honor yourself and children by finding balance and awareness as a parent. Bring your family honor by showing up as the best version of you as often as you can. Being honorable isn't about pleasing others or gaining outside admiration, it's about how you view and perceive yourself, and how you show up. Living with integrity and being true to yourself are huge stepping-stones to remember along the continuum of the parenting path. The umbrella of living with honor also encompasses remembering to be loyal, reliable, honest, dependable, and resilient in the process of parenting.

Parenting asks everything and more of you, being able to weather the storms and hard work will help you to build character and will lead to success if you stay the course and put in the effort that is required. Additionally, living with honor demonstrates to your child you are the rock and guiding light they need as they navigate their own course and their own experience. It teaches them you are the positive force they can rely on, as well as showing them you are living and breathing for a cause greater than yourself. You will inspire and uplift them when they need you most. If you are in a committed relationship while parenting, show your partner honor by being the other half and making them feel valued, heard, seen, and respected. Make time to tend to your partner and stay true to your relationship and the vows you took to one another. Be honorable to the process of walking hand in hand and heart to heart as you raise your family together.

Finally, if you are tackling parenting as a single parent then make sure to honor yourself and your journey by making time to tend to your spirit. This is so important. If you have no one rallying behind or beside you, then make sure you remind yourself just how incredible and worthy you are. It is hard enough raising a family when there are two parents sharing the load and involved, but I want to give a big shout out to all those single parents who are carrying the load solo. You are working towards your angel wings. Respect the role of being a single parent shouldering the whole load.

Appreciate and admire the work you do, and know that you are shaping and making such a difference for your child(ren), and it matters. How lucky and fortunate is your child for having a parent so committed to being there? So lucky. I bow to you. Make time for self-care and honor every part of you that feels in need.

KEEP DREAMING

If you can dream it, then you can certainly do it. What are your dreams in this life? Are you living them or working towards what really fulfills you? If not, then start! Life is a journey and one that is full of adventure and meant to be enjoyed, especially after having children. If certain ideas or plans seem out of reach, then perhaps rearrange the way you think about them and work towards making your dreams a reality. Life is such a beautiful gift and one that is meant to be enjoyed.

Being a parent doesn't mean you have to stop dreaming.

You can have your cake and eat it too. You can enjoy your family life and still make time to nurture and tenderly care for the parts of you that dream. Live a life that is less conventional, dream the most beautiful dream you can, and then start living it. I will remind you the only limiting factor in this equation is you. Shift priorities to see things come to fruition and more into alignment with what your heart and soul desire. If you are finding it hard to find bliss in your everyday, perhaps you are on the wrong path. Take time to reflect, journal, and meditate on what dreams are landing. In the deepest parts of you, you know where you are meant to be, so listen to this inner voice and find more joy. Dream your wildest dream and make it your reality.

Becoming a parent doesn't mean you can't continue to dream. Don't stop living because you've entered the family zone. Having a child doesn't equate with hitting the pause button, as there are still many ways to live a full and rich life while raising your young. I have heard many families over the years say that they can't do this or that because they have kids and my question would be, "why not?" Say that you love to travel…just because you have a child doesn't mean you can't still be adventurous–bring them with you! We started traveling with our boys when they were just a few months old, and I will always be grateful we did. Don't be afraid to re-define what your dreams and aspirations are once starting a family.

Make sure to tend to your dreams so your own heart doesn't get swept out to sea. Your heart is like a beautiful garden that needs tending, and if you forget to water your garden and pick the weeds, your garden won't grow as beautifully. Take care here and make time to dream and keep it light when you can. Make plans for the future and pencil in some merrymaking along the way, as this is crucial to tending to your own essence. Making your dreams a reality will make you a better parent, it will help you continue to expand and grow, and it will illuminate the parts of you that are meant to shine.

REMINDERS

Having daily reminders around your home is an incredible way to remember your consciousness as a parent. I personally use reminders all the time. I have different notes or pieces of art in our house that remind me to remember how to pause, give thanks, and remind myself of the right way to live and parent. I will share with you some of my favorites on my fridge:

"Let us be grateful to people who make us happy, they are the charming gardeners who make our souls blossom."
- Marcel Proust

"Listen to the wind, it talks. Listen to the silence, it speaks. Listen to your heart, it knows." - Native American

Proverb

"Love is the answer." - Unknown

"To enjoy good health, to bring true happiness to one's family, to bring peace to all, one must first discipline and control one's own mind." - Buddha

These are just a few examples, but you can get creative and put reminders anywhere in your space, if this serves. Putting reminders in places you frequent in or outside of your home are the best ways to engage with this. For example, utilize the fridge, bathroom mirror, closet, office, your laptop, inside your work bag or car visor. It also can be helpful to wear reminders such as jewelry, tucking a stone in your pocket (I am especially fond of rose quartz), or even a piece of clothing that helps remind you of how you want to live as you don that item in the morning. This way, you can see it or feel it throughout your day. Having a tactile reminder can be powerful medicine. The biggest takeaway here is to do what it takes to remember the right way to live, speak, and behave when raising your child and tending to your own heart in the process.

Every time I see a triple time on the clock–1:11 p.m., for example–I pause and put my hand on my heart, ground myself, and come into contact with my consciousness. This is an easy way for me to remember what I am doing, re-focus my attention, and find intention throughout the day.

Whatever works best as a daily reminder for you is encouraged. It could be seeing a butterfly, seeing a sign that you drive by on your way to work, a certain color or when you have your first cup of coffee or tea in the morning. Something to make you remember your consciousness and your joy spot as a parent is what is asked for here. This simple act can help you remember your intention, your promise to yourself to be the best parent you can be.

DEDICATION

Being dedicated as a parent is big. Being totally devoted to the process of raising your child and doing this with loyalty, integrity, honesty, sincerity, awareness, and love is the ultimate goal.

Think of this as being in service to your child(ren) during the 18 years you are blessed to have them in your home, under your roof. They are yours and you are theirs, and they really need you–the best version of you. Make this process a radiant one for both parties, this is possible and attainable.

Remind yourself this is the most important job you will ever have and remain steadfast to your post.

Being committed to the task at hand and having a firm, yet clear vision of your duty as a parent will help you remember how to be conscious, dedicated, and totally awesome as the pillar your kids need you to be.

I am truly dedicated to my children. They are beautiful spirits with so much to give. They make me crazy at moments, but even when I'm faced with something that feels challenging, I don't take my eye off the goal of being the constant they need. Being present and being the one they can count on means everything to me as a mom. When they forget to pack their lunch and call me from school, need me to read with them before bed, or need me to take them to hockey practice, I feel so grateful that I can be there to help support and guide them on their journey.

INTENTION

We've discussed intention, but let's re-visit as this is a critical point. What does it mean to live intentionally? How can we interlace more intention into daily life? To live with intention means being one with your life force. It means listening to that guiding voice inside that is there but often put on mute because the demands of daily life for most people are so overwhelming, especially for parents and caregivers. These demands can make it difficult to engage in being present and showing up in a way that is authentic and fully aligned with who you want to be. When your intentions are in alignment with how you want to be living and parenting, things naturally will fall into place. When there is misalignment, you are going to hit many more bumps in the road. This is a fairly simple recipe so be sure to bring intention to all that you do.

The most powerful impact intention can have is bringing one back to the present moment. When you are living in the present moment, it is much easier to be intentional with your words, gestures, and offerings to the world and your children. Living intentionally is a gift you give to yourself because you've set the expectation of how you want to show up for others as well as yourself. In doing so, you will be giving a gift to all you come into contact with. If you aren't living the life you are wanting to live, then make a change. Shift your reality to align with what your heart and mind desire and know is possible. In doing so, it will open channels that will forever change your course as well as your child's. Be fierce and live with intention; this will light your spirit up.

I am working hard to bring more intentionality to my family life every day. This is a conscious practice and one that requires constant tending. A simple way in which I practice bringing this to the table is carving out specific time for family activities. Some of our favorite family activities are taking walks together in the evening or on the weekends, watching a movie together where everyone is present and not distracted, reading a book where everyone sits to listen, playing catch or kickball in the yard, and making time to individually tend to our children at bedtime. I also work to make specific time that is dedicated to homework and really focusing on the task at hand so the boys can be prepared and organized for school…this one is a work in progress, ha! It doesn't really matter what the intentional activities or ideas are, just that you take time to check in on ways you can get more intentional in your life with your family. Carving out time that is meaningful and joyful is what is asked for.

SELF-CARE

Taking care of you in the process of raising your family is of utmost importance, especially when it comes to maintaining your **glow**. Self-care is not selfish. Self-care is what will give you the edge and support in being able to meet the best version of yourself and will help to sustain you in the work you do. Making self-care a priority in your life will change your life for the better. I am not talking about sneaking out to get a massage once a month or once every six months. That is great and can be helpful, but I am talking about practicing self-care *every* day. It doesn't have to take long, but you need to learn how to tend to yourself daily, even if it is five minutes that you devote to your personal wellness. If you can fit some of the bigger, bougie wellness treatments in on a regular basis, then rock on, this will help. For many, however, this is not an option, so your self-care might be as simple as rubbing a nice oil on your feet before bed after a long day, participating in a mindfulness activity daily, doing a face mask for yourself or with your child, doing some journaling, spending time in your garden, or spending time outside. Whatever fills your cup the most in life, tend to it on a regular basis. Taking time to tend to you will make you a better parent.

IMAGINATION

Imagination is the seed from which creativity and advancement can stem. When was the last time you used your imagination? This is not just some idea or notion that is only to be used by children. Imagination allows the human mind to continue expanding and reaching into areas not yet charted. It opens new pathways and pushes the boundaries of what we think is possible.

Imagination brings freedom and lays the foundation for inventiveness. It also allows room for personal growth and learning and helps prevent stagnation. Don't simply stand on the imagination of others for your inspiration. Be inspired, yes, but learn to turn on your own inner knowing and inner wilderness. Open your mind.

Set goals, make lists, make connections, and take the time to daydream on how to make your innovations come to life. Be resourceful. Don't limit what you think is possible, and perhaps even more importantly, don't let others limit what you think is possible. High five yourself if you have no one rallying behind you. If you do have a team surrounding you with love and validation, make sure you celebrate along the way. Breathe life into a new project or idea you've always been interested in but never thought was possible or had time for. The mind is so powerful; what you think and believe ultimately becomes your reality. Believe in your abilities and see what comes to fruition. You might just surprise yourself. Have fun. Be playful. Smile. Let your wildest imaginings come to life.

For me, I never had much time to practice using my imagination until I had children. Up until that point I had been too busy in school learning fundamentals, doing sports, working, or just being focused on the task at hand. The focus was more practical and external in nature for most of my life. When I had my children, my focus turned inward, and I had time at home in a way I had never experienced before. Sure, I was busy and hyper-focused on my babies, but I also learned what it meant to not have so many external distractions because I was often home alone with my children.

Before my boys started talking, I spent much of my time not talking with others and this started to open a gateway in my brain that allowed me to be much more imaginative and playful. I would come up with songs to sing to my children or imagine things with them that before I didn't have time to. It led to more creativity and personal satisfaction, and helped me rekindle a part of me that had never been truly nurtured. I felt like I was late to the party, but at least I finally arrived.

Getting imaginative was a personal blessing, but also a blessing for my children because it allowed me to share my imagination with them and took us on fun adventures, whether it was in a song, story, art project, or play. It was an opportunity to remember my own child-like center and not lose touch with that part of myself.

As you age, I believe that having a grasp and connection with the part of you that is still child-like and imaginative will serve you in keeping you feeling more youthful, more full of joy and wonder, and will help you live in the moment on much more regular basis. Make time to reconnect with the creative and imaginative side that lives within you, especially if you haven't visited that part of yourself in a long time. Put in the effort to bring your **glow** into full focus here; you will feel brighter, and your family will appreciate the special gifts you bring that are uniquely yours.

GET IN THE WATER

Water is a tremendous element for grounding and releasing energy, as well as energizing your system. I recommend getting in the water as much as possible as a parent as it is an incredible way to reset and nourish your mind, body, and spirit. It doesn't matter what water form is your favorite: a hot bath (I love to add Epsom salt & essential oils to mine), lake, ocean, hot spring, pool, creek, river, hot tub, cold plunge, etc. they are all incredible at helping you find relief and release. Natural bodies of water seem to offer the most healing and feeling of connection, but take whatever form is available to you and use it as often as possible. There is tremendous mind-body healing that happens when you submerge in the water. It takes you right into the present moment and allows you to let life's troubles or stresses wash away.

Dr. Wallace J. Nichols, a marine biologist, who wrote *Blue Mind: The Surprising Science that Shows how Being Near, In, On or Under Water Can Make You Happier, Healthier, More Connected and Better at What You Do,* speaks to the enormous benefits reaped by our minds and bodies when we spend time in, on, or near the water. Some of these benefits include experiencing calm, mindfulness, enhanced creativity, lower heart rate and breathing rate, and elevated and sustained happiness. He uses neurophysiological and behavioral brain testing to measure this, standing on science to back up the findings. This is something I've always felt about water, but to have science there to prove it is an added bonus.

Water is incredibly important to our family. We make special efforts to spend as much time in the water as possible. From the time our boys were babies, we taught and encouraged them to be in the water. They have grown up with a deep love and joy for playing in or on the water, and that makes my heart full. Our boys love all things water. We have prioritized being near water, especially since starting a family, and because of this they have spent much of their childhoods playing in lakes, rivers, streams, puddles, snow, the ocean…you get the idea. They especially love kayaking, surfing, swimming, skiing, and snowboarding. Really anything water related, and you can count them, and our whole family in.

Water has blessed my life in many ways, whether it is looking at water, submerging in the water or getting to recreate on it. I know that water has been a deeply healing and calming element in my life. I see and feel all the ways it has enhanced my path as a parent and as an individual; the gratitude I feel for water in all its forms is immeasurable. Consider making time to connect with this healing element as often as you can.

DATE NIGHTS

If you are in a relationship as a parent, I cannot express how important it is to take some time weekly or monthly to go out with your sweetheart. Being intentional about carving out sacred time for you to remember one another without your child is priceless, and also helps keep your foundation as a couple rock solid. When you are wearing the hat of a parent, you often present differently for your spouse or significant other than when it is just the two of you. This is just the reality of the shift in dynamics when you have children as part of the mix.

There are boundaries that need to be set, different emotions to factor in, competing needs, demands, routines, scheduled activities, or appointments, and all of these things have an impact on how you are able to show up for one another. If pillow talk and a smooch at the end of the day is all you are able to squeeze in during the week, then be grateful for that. If you have the luxury of more time, then maximize this and don't take one another for granted. Make sure you stay a team and tenderly care for the parts of each other that matter most, you know what that looks like for your other half. Be sensitive and be true.

Leave notes for one another, surprise each other with flowers or a token of your love, show each other you care not just on special occasions, but during the weekday grind. Don't forget to infuse romance and caring for each other and keep the flame alight through the twists and turns of being a conscious parent. If you've found yourself neglectful to your partner since starting a family, make the time to sit down and talk about ways to reboot your system and get that **glow** back.

CONTINUE LEARNING

Continuing to grow and learn once you become a parent helps you stay connected to your own personal feelings of fulfillment. Making time to seek out knowledge about subjects that interest you or satisfy the curious parts of your spirit will help you to parent from a happier and more well-rounded vantage point. Not only are you helping raise your family, but you are working towards meeting your own personal goals in parallel. When you can walk both paths in tandem, this helps strike a balance that keeps you feeling nourished and **glowing**. In the same vein, be cautious not to take on too many extracurriculars when you are in the thick of child rearing, as too much additional work can have the opposite effect you intend, so be sure to seek this out with care. You will learn your limits as you go, so touch base with yourself as often as is helpful.

Having a mindset of curiosity and the desire to continue to learn also will likely lead to boosting your confidence and help you acquire new skills or information that will support you on your path. Honestly, being a lifelong learner will support you in many ways and make you feel proud of who you are and what you've worked for. The other piece that I absolutely love about continuing to learn is it opens your mind to new perspectives and keeps you lighter as a human. It allows for more willingness to add to the bag you carry and also challenges you to keep building on what you already know. If your children witness you pursuing your dreams via learning, you are teaching them a form of leadership and encouraging them to pursue further education as they grow. What a tremendous gift you are giving yourself and your family as they bear witness to you growing your wings right in front of them.

I have found that I benefit immensely from continuing to learn. I have taken numerous different courses over the years since starting my family that have been deeply meaningful and fulfilling to me as a mom and individual. All have helped me on my path and have strengthened my conviction to show up and be all that I can be as a human and as a leader in my family. Some courses I have taken have been professionally driven, others have been hobby driven, and some infused with spirituality and growth. All have worked to weave their magic within me and make me stronger, more capable, more loving, and have taught me to live in better alignment with who I truly am and who I want to continue to be.

HUMOR

Humor can move mountains in your life, especially when

you are dealing with situations that don't always feel funny as a parent. While certain situations certainly are no laughing matter when raising a child, there are plenty of instances that you can turn something grumpy into something that brings a smile. The trick is in how you receive and perceive what's going on around you, and once again, choose to respond and not react.

Try not to take yourself too seriously. If you bring more laughter and lightheartedness to the table, you and your family will reap its benefits tenfold. For example, I recently was at the park and ran into an old acquaintance. She was pushing her young son on the swing and holding her dog at the same time, trying to juggle it all as parents do. We started chatting, and the more we were visiting, the more it was taking attention off of her son's needs. Eloquently, he cut in and said, "if you don't start pushing me, I will scream in your ear!" Well, that got her attention. I offered to hold her dog and gave her a minute to reconnect with her son. I also started giggling and said, "he is hilarious," to which she responded, "yes, to you!" We then both started to laugh. I appreciated how raw and real her son was, how he was clear about his needs as well, and how they needed to be met…or else.

I share this story because when you can infuse humor into the story of parenthood and acknowledge how insane it can be at times, it will lighten your perspective. When you take a minute to realize how volatile and intense your kids can be one moment and then right as rain the next, it gives greater depth into realizing how important it is to find your center point. When you learn to find your center point you can then be the base of the scales for your child as they bounce back and forth from one mood to the next, dealing with their ever-changing bodies and brains. Laughter is good medicine, so don't be afraid to break out a smile the next time your child does something or says something that you can't believe came out of such a tiny little body of perfection. Instead of getting mad or agitated, try laughing about the absurdity that is your life while you are walking the path of parenthood. Let humor be your healing balm and elixir for maintaining your radiance and your **glow**.

REFLECT

1. What does being radiant mean or look like to you?

2. How are you living intentionally? Are there any barriers to this process? If so, list them.

3. When it comes to bringing your **glow** to the surface, are you open to exposing this part of you as a parent? Are you willing to do what it takes to live your **glow**?

CHAPTER 13: LIVE YOUR PARENTING TRUTH

"The inspiration you seek is already within you. Be silent and listen."
- Rumi

It doesn't matter how you came into the role of being a parent, what matters is that you are a parent, doing the most important job there is. Period. Raising and shaping another human is as big as it gets. Be proud of who you are and the shoes you are walking in. You might not be proud of every moment or all the decisions you have made along the way, but own who you are, exactly as you are. You are perfection unfolding. There is no set timeline, so take the pressure off. Know you are right on time and exactly where you are meant to be.

DHARMA

What is the duty you came into this life to fulfill? If you are reading this book, parenting is likely a big part of your journey. Having a strong sense of values tied to consciousness will benefit you enormously as you parent. It will help you to live a life you are proud of, provide more clarity, and a stronger base from which to operate. Dharma has many definitions, but to me, dharma is ultimately about fulfilling the duty you are meant to in life or living your truth. What I especially like about the word and meaning behind dharma is that it reminds us that we came here to perform a task and learn.

Some of the greatest learning and deepest teachings have come from being a parent for me personally, and I'm guessing for many of you out there as well. Others may have a dual duty of parenting and a profession. I work hard to stay in touch with what my duty is here in life and when I feel like I am getting too far off my center point of what feels right, I try to shift gears and get back to my truth. It is a feeling I have in my bones. It is a knowing and a feeling beyond feeling.

There is also a peace and ease that comes from knowing I am fulfilling what I came here to fulfill, and being a mother is a big part of my personal journey. On the other hand, when I feel like I am deviating or not quite hitting my personal mark or doing my duty as best I can, I try to practice self-compassion and appreciate the parts of my path that feel less than because it's those moments of realization that can be pivotal for knowing where I am meant to be and where I am not. There is clarity that can land if you allow it.

We recently have been blessed with the opportunity for a collective parenting reset. With covid came the opportunity to look at systems that have not been serving the collective. We are experiencing a big time of flux, transition, and some growing pains as we rewrite what is acceptable and what is not as a global community, parenting and beyond. There is tragedy daily as you open the newspaper, glance at your phone, or watch television, but I am here to remind you that behind all that tragedy is so much beauty. You are surrounded by beauty; you need to remember to have eyes to see it and not forget that it exists.

The beauty and peace you seek as parents and as individuals lies within you and if you can remember to tap into that well spring of peace and ease daily, then you can share it with your children, family, neighbors, strangers, co-workers, and all others that cross your path. What a gift! Remember who you are and how beautiful you are; you are love, loved, and the giver of love. You can do, be, and seed anything you put your mind to. Don't forget this. You can live your truth and grow your infinite wisdom and be graceful and compassionate as a parent, all at the same time.

Weave this knowledge together and know there is no separation here. Parenting takes you apart and reassembles you bit by bit. This can be an exceptional experience if you are open to it and allow your very being to crack open and be made anew. It is truly a time of transformation, like that of a butterfly in chrysalis. Don't fight it, flow with it, and see the beauty that can emerge if you allow spaciousness and unpredictable unfolding to occur. The more you fight this process, the more struggle you will experience, so let go and swim with the current. Don't continue to swim upstream.

Living your parenting truth starts with acknowledging you need to put the time into making contact with your conscious and whole self on a daily basis, not just when you go on a retreat, read a parenting book, every now and then, or when it feels most convenient. It is about waking up to your reality and living it with determination, intention, love, dedication, and with a drive that will carry you through any storm or blue sky. It is about living from this place *every day*. This is not an easy path but the more you practice, the easier it will become. It can and will become second nature if you want it to be. You can bring anything you want into your reality, so if becoming a conscious parent is a priority to you, then make it so. Live it, breathe it, walk it, and share it with your family.

BE OF SERVICE

As a parent, you have been placed in the awesome role of

being in service to your child. You are in service and needed around the clock. Not only are you in service to your family, but you also have the ability to teach your children as they grow about what it means to be of service to others.

Living from a place of service can move mountains. It can help foster deep personal satisfaction, knowing you are making a difference for others. Service helps the collective, builds responsibility, and helps improve self-esteem. It matters.

One of my personal practices is to shoot conscious arrows of love when I am out in the community. For example, I will see someone on the street who appears to be in need in one way or another, and I energetically send them love. I shoot my metaphoric arrow of love and see this love surrounding them, bringing them peace, safety, and support. I also will do this if I am in a setting where I am witnessing someone who appears to be under a lot of stress or struggling in one way or another. There are ways to be of service that don't always require physical action or interaction.

Energy is energy and can be shared in many different ways. Be creative and thoughtful here about how you wish to share your energy with others. You can make a difference, even if it isn't tangible or visible for others to see.

Out in the world, different ways I have lived and manifested serving others into being is by volunteering in a soup kitchen and food bank, buying groceries for the person behind me in line at the grocery store (this is one of my favorite offerings during the holiday season), bringing food or donating money to homeless individuals, leaving a generous tip for those in the service industry, bringing cookies and a kind note to the local police station, picking up trash in the community, and bringing in food for teachers at our local schools. The final example I want to share here is often after our family goes out to eat, if we see someone in need on the street, we will offer them our leftovers or offer to get them a meal. The kids have helped us with this, so it is leaving a positive impression on them to help others in need, and to have eyes to see those that many times go 'unseen.' We talk about it, we are living it, and having follow-through.

One experience that really touched my heart was bringing a box of food to a homeless man during the height of the Covid-19 pandemic. The streets were bare, businesses were shut down, and there was just an eerie feeling to the environment during the tough time we all were collectively experiencing. This man clearly hadn't bathed or been able to practice self-care for an awfully long time and was living in conditions that are unimaginable to most of us. I wanted to make a difference for him, even if it was a small gesture.

I got out of my car at sunset and found him on the sidewalk trying to make a bed for the night and offered him a box of food. He just looked at me with his matted hair and soiled clothes and said, "thank you ma'am." There was something in his eyes that just pierced right through me. He was emitting such tenderness, rawness, tragedy, and pain that stirred something in my soul. I remember leaving and going home that night, but as I lay in bed getting ready to go to sleep I saw him again in my mind, this time in a different light. I imagined him wearing all white, a beautiful suit of linen. He was barefoot, clean, and glowing. He was smiling and joyful, the heartache and hardship was gone. I sat down before him to wash his feet and show my respect. It was an image that I will never forget. Honestly, even writing this makes the tears well up. I once had been at a retreat where there was an offering to have my feet washed, not like a pedicure, but something more meaningful and intentional, a deep offering. For whatever reason, this past experience reappeared.

How often do you cross paths with others so acutely in need in your community and yet you do not do anything, or pretend not to see what is right in front of you. This is not a guilt trip but an opportunity to go deeper, see with eyes full of compassion and work to make more of a difference wherever you can. If we all start doing small, meaningful deeds, those small acts of kindness add up. Imagine the world we could possibly create if we remember how to care for one another.

You may be wondering how this story of a homeless man is relevant to becoming a conscious parent. I will reiterate that teaching and showing your children what this looks like and how to give and be of service is the most beautiful gift you can give them. Not only are you living your **glow** here, but you are helping others **glow** in the process, and that is my personal definition of ultimate success. When you give, is when you truly receive.

REFLECT

1. Are you living your parenting truth? What does this look or feel like to you? Write an outline of what your dharma is.

2. How are you serving others in your daily life? Are you open to teaching your child(ren) about being in service to others?

3. What is one way you can share your energy in a positive way, with your family or others?

CHAPTER 14: FINALE

"Body like a mountain, heart like the ocean, mind like the sky,"
- Dogen

During the course of writing this book I had a moment where I was asked to **stop.** I was in full blown writing and editing mode when I began having pain in my right breast. This is not a symptom I have ever had, and it was totally foreign to me. I didn't pay too much attention to it at first, but when it persisted for two weeks and was waking me up at night when I would roll over, I decided it was time to tell my husband and seek medical evaluation to help put my mind at ease. I am healthy and figured everything was probably fine, but wanted a second opinion, so I went to a walk-in clinic for a basic screening.

I was hoping to get a quick mammogram and then call it a night, but when I went in and described my symptoms the woman working that evening told me I needed a more thorough work-up and that she wouldn't do the mammogram. It was not going to be as simple as I was expecting it to be. Feeling unsettled with the news and not getting immediate results, I went home feeling uneasy. I ended up seeing my primary care provider about a week later. She ordered me a mammogram, which I was thankfully able to get in for later that week. There was a radiologist present to do an ultrasound if needed. This was my first mammogram ever. I am 38 and figured I still had plenty of time before I needed one. It wasn't really on my radar.

When I went in to finally get my mammogram, about four days after my visit with my primary care provider, I was starting to feel nervous. This is not a feeling normally present in my life. I initially had hoped for quick results but had to wait about another week and a half before finally being fully evaluated. The woman who helped me that morning was incredibly kind. We took a couple sets of x-rays on both breasts, and she said she was going to have the radiologist take a look and if he saw anything he would do an ultrasound.

"Hang tight," she said. Again, I was being evaluated for pain in my right breast. When she came back in the room she said, "The doctor would like to do an ultrasound on your left breast."

"What? The pain is in my right breast, are you sure it's the left?"

"Yes, it is the left one he would like to ultrasound."

At that point I was feeling very unsettled with the news. She led me to another room where an ultrasound tech was waiting for me. He did the ultrasound and then a few minutes later the radiologist came into the room, saying he had found a mass that was of concern. He said it looked like a benign tumor, but he couldn't be certain. The pain I was experiencing in my right breast, he said, was related to cysts that were of no concern. He recommended I have the mass in my left breast closely monitored every six months, and also added that I have very dense breast tissue which increases my risk of breast cancer. With that, he sent me on my way.

I was a bit shell shocked when I got home. I went in for one symptom but what they found was linked to something else completely. The news I received was totally unexpected. What do you do with news like that? *Is it cancer? Is it not? Should I be worried, or should I put it out of my mind and power on as I always have?* There weren't conclusive results to what he found and the symptom I initially went in to be seen for wasn't a problem.

In the midst of trying to process this news privately, I found myself making breakfast for my kids one morning and starting to break down because this experience was asking me to look at my life with a larger lens. One of my sons asked me, "what's wrong mom?" And I just smiled, gave him a hug, and brushed it off. I didn't want my kids to worry. Our time is fleeting here, and I began to wonder if my time was going to be limited based on the uncertain news I had just received. I also was worried I wouldn't be there for my children when they needed me. Even though I had no conclusive evidence of cancer, these were the thoughts swirling. A short time after receiving these results and doing a little personal research I decided to request a biopsy so I could know definitively what exactly the mass was. Sitting, waiting, and watching the mass didn't feel like the best option for me, and I felt I had too much at stake with my family to wait it out. Not knowing was eating at me. This was the perfect opportunity for me to practice how to still my mind, body, and spirit.

This experience of not knowing and being in close contact with the preciousness of life helped me to re-evaluate priorities in my life in short order. During this time frame, we pulled our boys out of school for a day and took them skiing. For this one day we stopped the routine and instead created our own. We found joy in each other's company and let go of the to-do's. We just played and let the snow and sunshine lead the way that day. It was joyful.

This experience helped me remember that so many people go through things in life that they keep to themselves, many things which are tough. Yet they are asked to rise in the morning, tend to their duties and keep putting one foot in front of the other, often while putting on a brave face and pretending all is well. The human experience and parenthood ask everything and more of you, and the road isn't always easy. I've learned these tender moments in life can help you see things more clearly.

To rewind, since waiting and watching the mass closely wasn't the best option for me, I chose to have this mass biopsied. Thankfully, I was able to get on the radiologist's schedule relatively quickly, and he actually found a second mass when I was in that morning for the exploratory biopsy. Soon after, I had a follow-up and the final results showed neither mass was cancerous. I had a huge sigh of relief, and felt deep gratitude that my body was free of this devastating disease that cruelly takes so many.

The four to five week timespan of being on this rollercoaster of emotions gave me a deeper perspective on life. It reminded me how I want to live and show up for myself and others, as well as re-affirmed how being intentional and practicing mindfulness in my life has supported and transformed me for the better. Being conscious in good times and in the bad will help you find your center and work from a place of more peace and intentionality.

FINAL REMARKS

Parenting is a serious rite of passage. You can read about parenting, you can study it and have lots of ideas about what parenting is and what it is not, or even how it should look, but until you are living and breathing what it means to be a parent, you really have no idea. I mean that with the utmost sincerity and kindness. It is very much a lived experience. An experience that will forever change you from the ground up. My deepest intention is that this parenting framework will help parents come into the alignment (mind, body, spirit, environment) they've always dreamed of being in, that it will allow for more intentional, gentle, joyful, mindful, and graceful living for parents and children alike.

I am a deeply private person, and some of the sharing I have done in this book was hard for me to write. It exposes some of my soft underbelly which isn't all together comfortable. It feels vulnerable in many ways, and yet I have chosen to share because I have a deep desire to help others. I genuinely want to make a difference for parents and support them on their journey. I want other parents to see that we all have "stuff," no matter what it looks like on the outside. We all carry different burdens and are asked different things in life.

I urge you to honor who you are and learn to love every part of you, the individual, the mother, the father, the auntie, the uncle, the sister, the brother, the boss, the employee, the perpetual student of life, and the child. Sharing some of my struggles and my joys as a mother has been a personally transformative experience…cathartic even. I hope you will honor yourself enough to learn to live with more self-compassion, especially the parts that still need work. We all need work, and we are all learning. Remember that when you gaze into your son or daughters' eyes, when you pass strangers on the street, or even when you look at yourself in the mirror. We are all in this together, so let's tread a little lighter and offer more support for one another as we continue on.

I often think of the lyrics of John Lennon's famous song, *Imagine*, "imagine all the people livin' for today." I am ever the optimist, and I believe this is possible. What a gift we could give ourselves, our children, and the world: to live for today. To consciously stop living from the past or for the future, but living and showing up for the now so that we can be totally in touch with what is right in front of us. To show and teach our children that it is possible to live in the present and not live with so many distractions. Even when things get chaotic, scary, and busy, remember you always have a choice of how you arrive to a situation. Even in the midst of madness, you can always remember to breathe and meet your madness with joy and courage to keep going. You are so much stronger, braver, and more resilient than perhaps you realize.

Know that reading this book will not make you a perfect parent. These are tools and inspirations to draw from daily or as often as you can remember. They have helped me and continue to help me on this parenting walk I am on. Days I forget to open my toolbox, I feel it and so do my kids. When I remember, it's really amazing the difference, it is night and day actually. I'm remembering how to parent in a conscious way much more often than I used to. Whatever tools or platform you choose to operate from, make sure you infuse it with love. This recipe will never steer you in the wrong direction.

To reflect on where we've been…this parenting journey is about learning how to **stop** and pause long enough to do some self-assessment on where you are to date. It is about working to **drop** the drama, trauma, or realities in your life that are not serving you as a parent and individual. It's about learning to **grow** by leaning into positive habits and ultimately practicing living your **glow** in the world and with your family. Don't skip steps in this framework. It is important you start at the foundation, **stop**, and work your way up. For example, if you jump in after reading this book and just try to **grow**, you haven't put the work into really cementing and repairing who you are as an individual or worked on dropping habits that may not be serving you as a parent.

Don't neglect these personal parts of who you are and where you've been, as they may come to the surface at a later date and call for your attention, and not always in the most ideal way. Make time to intentionally tend to each of the four pillars and be systematic as you work your way through these teachings. Remember to honor your whole being, the great along with the not so great. A big take away from the Stop, Drop, Grow, & Glow Method is to learn to parent from a place of wholeness and intentionality and then bring your teachings to life with your family daily. Take your time and don't rush the process. Things will unfold as they are meant to, trust in that.

Utilizing the Stop, Drop, Grow, & Glow Method will set you on the path for parenting that is imbued with consciousness. It will elevate your personal experience with parenting and an added bonus is that it will actually elevate your child's experience as well. It will help you tend to the parts of you that perhaps need a major overhaul and will open doors that maybe have never been opened before. Getting real with who you are and how you show up, both for yourself and others, will have positive lasting benefits that hopefully you carry forever. Peering into your own center and cleaning house on many levels will work to free you as a person and as a parent. Get to work and start reimagining what parenting is and what parenting can be. Draw from my offerings but write your own rules about what family and parenting is all about and start today.

Finally, I wanted to address the reflection questions throughout this book. I did this on purpose, and for a reason. When you are in the midst of parenting, you are asked to really look at who you are and how you show up, whether you want to or not; it's in your face every day. If you don't pause to question where you are, where you've been, how to show up in the now, and where you are headed, it makes it tough to see the whole picture and see how you fit into it. I've learned and continue to learn many lessons as a mother. I've found that while I've experienced different emotions, sensations, and realities at different stages in life, being a parent has been the most significant and impactful to date. I believe this to be true because I am no longer just working on "me," but I am working on shaping other humans which has much deeper implications. Prioritize making time to reflect, as it will help you and will make a difference in your life.

I will leave you with this, fellow parents…marry your consciousness with parenting, and everything you do for that matter. Live intentionally and align yourself with your values and priorities so you can help your child discover theirs. Dig deep, love hard, and lean on joy to guide your way. Parent like you mean it and learn to live your **glow**.

AN EXTENSION OF GRATITUDE

I want to give special thanks to my husband and four sons for supporting me on my journey in writing this book. The gratitude, love, and appreciation I feel for each of you is endless. Thank you.

I want to thank my father and sister for their blessings and support in sharing part of our family story. I love you both dearly.

I want to thank Lauren Eckhardt and Allison Buehner at Burning Soul Press for their support, words of encouragement, professionalism, and kindness on this book writing journey. I have sincerely treasured working with you both and I have grown immensely since we first began.

I want to extend thanks to all my friends and family for their support and time. Especially, Amy Pelloquin, M.D., Kay Kramer, OTR/L, CHT, Deanna Mylander, William Mylander, Constance Swenson, and Emilie Johnston.

I want to thank all of the beautiful parents who shared and added richness and insight to The Parenting 12.

Lastly, I want to thank all of my mentors and teachers over the years. I bow to your gorgeous wisdom.

REFERENCES

Better Sleep for a better you. Sleep Foundation. (2023, March 3). https://www.sleepfoundation.org/

Centers for Disease Control and Prevention. (n.d.). Centers for Disease Control and Prevention. https://www.cdc.gov/

Centers for Disease Control and Prevention. (2022, June 2). *How much physical activity do adults need?* Centers for Disease Control and Prevention. https://www.cdc.gov/physicalactivity/basics/adults/index.htm

Collaborative Problem Solving®. Think. (2023, April 27). https://thinkkids.org/cps-overview/

Cronkleton, E. (2022, March 29). *Vata dosha: Diet, meaning, characteristics, and more.* Medical News Today. https://www.medicalnewstoday.com/articles/vata-dosha

The Editors of goop. (n.d.). *What is conscious uncoupling?*. Goop. https://goop.com/wellness/relationships/conscious-uncoupling-2/

Evans, O. G., & Olivia Guy (2023, May 1). *Hypothalamic-pituitary-adrenal (HPA) Axis & the*

Stress Response. Simply Psychology. https://www.simplypsychology.org/hypothalamic-pituitary-adrenal-axis.html

Grunwald, T. (Ed.). (2023, March). *Growth hormone deficiency (for parents)*. KidsHealth. https://kidshealth.org/en/parents/gh-deficiency.html

How much water should you drink? Harvard Health. (2022, May 15). https://www.health.harvard.edu/staying-healthy/how-much-water-should-you-drink

Hormonal imbalance: Causes, symptoms & treatment. Cleveland Clinic. (n.d.). https://my.clevelandclinic.org/health/diseases/22673-hormonal-imbalance%20%20%20%20

Ingraham, C. (2021, November 25). *Divorce is actually on the rise, and it's The baby boomers' fault*. The Washington Post. https://www.washingtonpost.com/news/wonk/wp/2014/03/27/divorce-is-actually-on-the-rise-and-its-the-baby-boomers-fault/

Kaputk. (2022, December 27). *Box breathing benefits and techniques*. Cleveland Clinic. https://health.clevelandclinic.org/box-breathing-benefits/

Leproult, R., & Van Cauter, E. (2010). Role of sleep and sleep loss in hormonal release and metabolism. *Endocrine development*, *17*, 11–21. https://doi.org/10.1159/000262524

MacMillan, C. (2022, August 1). *Is my sunscreen safe?* Yale Medicine. https://www.yalemedicine.org/news/is-sunscreen-safe

Mayo Foundation for Medical Education and Research. (2022, April 29). *A beginner's guide to meditation*. Mayo Clinic. https://www.mayoclinic.org/tests-procedures/meditation/in-depth/meditation/art-20045858

Nichols, W. J. (2015). *Blue Mind: The Surprising Science That Shows How Being Near, In, On, or Under Water Can Make You Happier, Healthier, More Connected, and Better at What You Do*. Back Bay Books.

Puberty: Stages for Boys & Girls. (2021). https://my.clevelandclinic.org/health/articles/22192-puberty

Reef safe sunscreens / reef friendly sunscreens. BADGER. (n.d.). https://www.badgerbalm.com/pages/coral-reef-safe-sunscreen

Scott, S. B., Rhoades, G. K., Stanley, S. M., Allen, E. S., & Markman, H. J. (2013). *Reasons for Divorce and Recollections of Premarital Intervention: Implications for Improving Relationship Education*. National Center for Biotechnology Information. https://www.ncbi.nlm.nih.gov/pmc/

Sleep and disease risk. Sleep and Disease Risk | Healthy Sleep.

(2022).
https://healthysleep.med.harvard.edu/healthy/matters/consequences/sleep-and-disease-risk

Somatheeram - Ayurvedic Health Resort: Kerala, India - traditional and authentic. Somatheeram Ayurvedic Health Resort. (n.d.). https://somatheeram.org/en/

Stepler, R. (2020, July 27). *Led by Baby Boomers, divorce rates climb for America's 50+ population*. Pew Research Center. https://www.pewresearch.org/short-reads/2017/03/09/led-by-baby-boomers-divorce-rates-climb-for-americas-50-population/

N. O. and A. A. (2018, November 1). *Sunscreen chemicals and coral reefs*. Skincare Chemicals and Marine Life. U.S. Department of Commerce. https://oceanservice.noaa.gov/news/sunscreen-corals.html

U.S. Department of Health and Human Services. (n.d.). *College drinking*. National Institute on

Alcohol Abuse and Alcoholism. https://www.niaaa.nih.gov/publications/brochures-and-fact-sheets/college-drinking

ABOUT THE AUTHOR

Holly Swenson, BSN, RN, is the author of *Stop, Drop, Grow, & Glow*, a revolutionary book on conscious parenting. Formally trained as a registered nurse and a mother to four sons, she brings her wisdom and lived experience to the forefront of her writing as a means to help others on their parenting and personal path. She has found that beyond being a mother and devoted wife, writing and sharing with others is one of her deepest purposes in life and it is the ultimate motivation for her to help uplift and encourage fellow beings around the world. Internal and external change is possible, one word at a time. That is her favorite part about being an author; opening a door that may forever bring more peace, healing, and clarity to the reader. When she is not writing at home or in her favorite tea shop, she spends her time with her husband and boys enjoying the outdoors, gardening, doing yoga, traveling, giving back, and living life to the fullest. She also writes a wellness blog, moonrisingdesigns.blog as a simple offering to others.

Please visit her online at www.liveyourglow.live.

Made in United States
Orlando, FL
08 November 2023